Paschal Journey

Reflections on Psycho-Spiritual Growth

Patrick J. Brennan

Deacon Guy A. Colella
4/92

THE THOMAS MORE PRESS
CHICAGO, ILLINOIS

ISBN 0-88347-267-8

Contents

For Kate and Katie:
The Foundation and the Hope

Introduction

This book is kind of a journal of my spirit or soul, over the past year or so. I believe that each day, month, year, and season of life lived is a share in the "mystery of Christ crucified." "An absurdity and stumbling block," Paul says of the paschal mystery in the first chapter of the first letter to the Corinthians. But to those of us "called," we experience in our sharing in the life, death, and resurrection of Jesus, the very "power" and "wisdom" of God, at work in the ordinariness of our lives.

These pages represent issues I have dealt with recently as I have shared Christ's journey from life experience to cross, to empty tombs, over and over again. Among them are: the need for greater gentleness; starting over after a defeat; appreciating each moment of life; holding on in hope during life's difficult moments; the importance of the human will in growth; becoming child-like; the importance of self-sacrificial love; the need for the Church to more willingly realize it is in a life-death-resurrection passage; the power of addictions in our culture; the conviction of a Higher Power who can free us from these various addictions; commitments; overcoming fear; loss; grief; reconciliation; rediscovering joy; re-gaining a sense of being at

Patrick J. Brennan

home in the world; discernment; God as comfort and challenge, and others.

I hope that my wonderings will help you in your paschal journey, your passage from life through death to new life—a mystery at work in us over and over again until we finally shed our physical selves to become totally Spirit.

I designed the book so that after each chapter there are journal questions that can be used for individual reflection or small group discussion, if some are discovering the richness of small, intentional base communities.

I am grateful to John Sprague, Joel Wells, Todd Brennan, and the late Dan Herr for their patience and encouragement. I thank also, Dawn Mayer, my associate, who read and edited parts of the book. And I owe special thanks to Sarah Tuohy who typed the bulk of the manuscript.

Patrick J. Brennan

Chapter One

On Becoming Gentle

It's human nature to want to retaliate, hurt back when hurt, use power against someone who is over-powering us. One of Jesus's challenges to us is non-retaliation in the face of power, hurt, and aggression. In a world of fierce independence, aggression and competition, he sounds at odds with common wisdom when he says: "You have heard it said, 'An eye for an eye, a tooth for a tooth.' But I say . . . offer no resistance to one who is evil. When someone strikes you on your right cheek, turn the other one to him as well. . . . You have heard you should love your neighbor and hate your enemy. But I say to you love your enemies, and pray for those who persecute you" (Matthew 5: 38-45).

Transcending Human Nature

THIS orientation toward non-aggression is displayed at the end of Jesus's life. Matthew's depiction of his arrest in the Garden of Gethsemane tells of someone accompanying Jesus coming forward, and cutting off the ear of the high priest's servant. Jesus says "Put your sword back into its sheath . . . all who take the sword will perish by the sword" (Matthew 26:52).

Patrick J. Brennan

Jesus's posture toward those who would hurt him was non-aggression and gentleness. Contemporary folks would wonder about the long-range efficacy of such a life style. As Thomas Hart writes in *To Know and Follow Jesus,* this selfless, gentle person spent his few adult years helping, healing, and liberating people. Others, jealous and power-motivated "got him for it." His gentleness resulted in his death. Contemporary society would be skeptical about Jesus's non-aggression: Look what it did for him. I really had to wrestle with his witness and invitation to gentleness in my own life recently.

The Best of Times, The Worst of Times

Recently I found myself being my worst self and my best self, or at least a better self. The worst self had to do with my car—less than a year old, a mid-size, mid-price car. Nonetheless, it still cost more than my parents' entire home when they bought it in 1950. At first glance, it was just a little annoyance, some of the new-fangled computer things and powered gadgets failed to work. I called the dealer where I bought it.

"Oh, that just sounds like a fuse! You can change it yourself. The area to work on is under the steering wheel," was the response I received.

I gave the old under the steering wheel routine about fifteen minutes. It became ever more apparent to me why I entered ministry, and not mechanics. I could not fix it. But I did not panic. If it was only a fuse, the service station people could handle it the next day.

10

PASCHAL JOURNEY

I dropped this relatively new car off at the service station on a Tuesday. Within one hour, I received a phone call from the man who usually works on my car.

"Father Brennan, you don't have a fuse problem—you have approximately three inches of water between the carpet in your car and the bottom the chassis. You better pick it up and bring it back to the dealer. There's got to be a structural defect in the car that's allowing water to accumulate where it shouldn't. The three inches of water has rotted out most of your wiring. This is the cause of your electrical problems."

I was stunned—a new car—supposedly, the state of the art machine—rotting due to a structural defect! "How much would re-wiring and repair cost?" I asked the service man.

"Oh, it's a pretty slow, expensive process—anywhere from $1,700 to $2,000!"

I was becoming enraged at the injustice heaped on me. I entered a contract in good faith, believing I was getting a decent product. Now I was being told two thousand dollars was being added to an already bloated bill, for a mistake that was made at the factory. I immediately brought the car back to the dealer from whom I had bought it.

His first question to me was "How many miles on this?" "Twenty-one thousand," I sheepishly replied. "Oh, too bad," he said, "it's out of warranty—12,000 miles." "But's its less than a year old," I countered. "Doesn't matter," he replied. "The warranty is for 12,000 miles or one year—whichever comes first. But

11

maybe the manufacturer will give you some sort of a deal."

"Some sort of a deal?" I wondered. Why should I be penalized for something that happened while the car was being made? The dealer's service manager wanted to hurry me along. "Your car will be fixed in a couple of days."

A couple of days passed, and I still had not heard anything. In fact, four days passed. On the fifth day, I called the service department. I was told it would be three or four more days. At the end of a complete week, I was told it would be another week. Approaching the two week period of "car hospitalization," I really became incensed. The present problem was that they could not find a new rug to put in the car; they were afraid to put the old one back in for fear of shorting out the wires again with a damp rug. It seemed incredible to me that finding a carpet for a car less then a year old could be so difficult. My paranoid self began to suspect that there were other problems. I also decided to "play hard ball." The man who usually received my calls continued to be annoyingly vague about what was happening with the car. All the while I was using borrowed cars. The volume and nasty tone of my threats became greater.

"I'm writing the consumer division of the manufacturer of this car. I'm contacting a lawyer. I'll stop payment on the car."

The service man was definitely a Type-B personality. All he would say is "Do whatever you want!"

PASCHAL JOURNEY

On about the 16th day I talked to another man in the service department. As I was about to launch into my multiple threats about litigations, he stopped me. "We have been a terrible service department. I'm doing my best to improve the quality of our service. I assure you, I will look into this personally." I was disarmed. There was no emergency anymore. Someone admitted there was some truth in my allegations. Before my "power" had been met with "greater power," or indifference. When my anger or power was met with concern and gentleness, my negative emotions were transformed into gentleness. I wanted to punch someone, but suddenly there was no one to punch.

The encounter with this gentle man reminded me of something I had read about the martial arts. A martial arts expert encouraged people learning about self defense, to not push back when pushed, but rather go with your opponent's push. Likewise if pulled, do not resist, he taught, rather go with the pull. Not resisting a push or a pull disarms one's opponent, and puts one in a fresh position of countering such an attack.

Power and Aggression

Many more people adhere to the power-aggression model of living than to Jesus's simplicity and gentleness. Carol Gilligan, writing in *In a Different Voice*, speaks of how most Western society is patterned on a male-skewed hierarchical/power model. Historically women have been the victims of systemic injustice in

Patrick J. Brennan

our social systems. We see mirrored in the abuse or misuse of women in our social structures, the suffering of the gentle Christ. Heretofore, women seemed to have been socialized more toward a gentleness, relationship-oriented thrust in life, as Jesus was. Hilary Lips, in *Women, Men and the Psychology of Power,* speaks of the male experience of power as the need for dominance over other men and women. Males apparently have a greater need for dominance than females. Some would say this is biologically determined, the result of evolution. Others says this is socially conditioned or a learned response to life. Traditionally, female power has been experienced in weaving and nurturing webs of relationships. This is not to say that many women cannot hold positions of power—translated as existential authority and life-giving. In fact many already do. But true women's liberation certainly does not resemble taking on the traditional trappings of the male-style of power. That would be a deterioration of the evolution of the female. No, women wisely are learning to assume positions of life-giving authority without the need for dominance-power, and without losing their touch with the relational.

Dominance-style power is an undertow in other dimensions of life, too. Often conflictual relationships in marriage and family (in most relationships of any kind, in fact) are due to one or more people playing power games in a relationship. Sociologist-minister Anthony Campolo said with eloquence at a gathering

14

at Chicago's Holy Name Cathedral that people in need of power are incapable of love. Campolo said the place of greatest love was the cross. On the cross, Jesus experienced what Paul referred to as *kenosis,* a total emptying out of self, ego needs, power. When we hear Christ's admonition to take up the cross, we are not being called to some sort of self-punitive extracurricular activity that is to be added to other burdens and struggles of life. No, the challenge put to us is, "Can you love like this, without power, as he did?"

With the advent of parent effectiveness seminars, some twenty years ago, lead by Carl Rogers and Thomas Gordan, it has become quite evident that power and aggression do not work well between parent and child. A parent who thinks good parenting involves heavy doses of dominance and power, often pushes the child to rebellion or other acting out behaviors. The goal of parenting is to constantly redefine and re-shape the parent-child relationship to assure the adult is (in an ongoing way) an authority (an author, a life giver), a mentor (teacher or guide), or as psychiatrist David Elkind says *(The Hurried Child, All Grown Up and No Place to Go)* a marker for children and adolescents (someone who points the way). I have seen so many children and teens become in fact more problematic in their behavior when power or aggression has been too often used on them. What is true of the parent-child relationship has parallels in teacher-child relationships.

In the Church we have seen power misused, abused

15

Patrick J. Brennan

and misinterpreted. The early experiences, in the first centuries of Christianity, of communities gathering around the presence of the Risen Lord, quickly gave way in the Church to a vertically operating hierarchy that resembled the pagan structures of the societies in which the Church existed. That distorted view of power has extended to our own day, as we experience renewed, though hopelessly flawed efforts by the Church to hold on to vertical power. In *The Church in the Midst of Creation,* priest-missionary Vincent Donovan writes that the hallmark of the vertically hierarchical church is an organzation wherein everything must be controlled by a central location, standardized, synchronized, and routinized. Donovan thinks this model of Church is rapidly coming unglued. Nonetheless it is still real, and providing a negative, painful experience of Church for many. Any thinking, feeling human being has to have the feeling of being "in between the times." The *National Catholic Reporter U.S. Catholic, America, Commonweal, The London Tablet,* and other popular Catholic periodicals have been looking critically at the huge Catholic population worldwide, and the phenomenon of Eucharistless communities. The latter is due to vertical dominance-power structures not even being willing to enter into serious dialogue regarding married clergy or women priests. The hierarchy's compulsive adherence to its inadequate structures and personnel for evangelization are literally pushing the spiritually seeking among the adolescent, young adult, adult and immigrants into the hands of proselytizers and evangelical groups.

Loughlan Sofield and Carroll Juliano speak of the tension between a power model and a collaborate model of ministry in their book *Collaborative Ministry*. The hierarchical model of Church militates against collaborative ministry, which identifies, releases, uses and unifies the charisms of all of the people of God. Even in settings where Vatican II—renewal jargon is used, there is often existential reluctance to break out of power models to true collaboration in ministry.

The Snowstorm — Practicing A New Skill

The memory of being dealt with gently by the one service department representative, or someone neither pushing nor pulling back, and of how it changed me, was still fresh in my mind when I received an angry phone call from one of my graduate students at Loyola University's Institute of Pastoral Studies in Chicago. After a new record snowstorm, I had cancelled my weekly class in evangelization. I did this on the recommendation of the school administration, since a phone call effort revealed only two students could make the class, with the aftermath of the snow and ice.

But one student certainly wanted to come. And he was the phone call I referred to earlier. This was his mind-set: he invested time and money in the class; and he expected it to happen. If he could be there, why couldn't I be there, and the other students. His tone was quite angry: "I'm getting the feeling that you're

Patrick J. Brennan

not committed to this class, to Loyola, that you don't want to be with us!" I immediately grew defensive, and if I had released what was on the tip of my tongue, it would have sounded something like this: "Are you crazy? We had a major snowstorm last night. It's dangerous to be out in this weather. Most normal students would welcome some free time — to rest or catch up on reading!" But I bit my tongue, and re-arranged the words in my head, and then I spoke: "I'm sorry you feel the way that you do. I want to reassure you that I'm committed to you, the class, and Loyola. I just agreed with the administration that it is rather dangerous to be out today. I promise I will gladly make-up the time and material missed however I can — even if that involves a one-on-one tutorial."

I could sense the student who was calling wanted to have someone to lash out at, to punch. But I had done to him what the kind, communicative service man did to me. Gentleness had again transformed aggression into gentleness. He backed down, apologized for his tone, and agreed to call if he needed the extra help.

Conclusion

You get back what you dish out, I guess. Power, in that worst, aggressive sense of the term begets more power and aggression. This is true not only in consumer service manager, teacher-student relationships. It is true also in marriage, in parenting, at work, in friendship or any other such attempt at ministry. The

18

least effective mode of relating is power; power is a love-blocker. The cross of Jesus Christ is a challenge to each of us to go through the necessary interior emotional re-arrangements to approach each other with gentleness rather than power.

When Jesus encourages us to pray for our enemies, he may be asking us to pray for someone under our own roof, at our own table, or with whom we are in a primary kind of relationship. In fact, to accomplish some of what Jesus invites us to, like not returning aggression for aggression, requires a great deal of prayer, a discipline of prayer that slowly, gradually changes a "power-aggression" consciousness. To become a gentle person requires that we engage in a *process* of "being perfected," says Jesus; so that gradually we more and more resemble the Father who *is* perfect.

Robert Fulghum, in his bestseller *All I Really Need to Know I Learned in Kindergarten,* articulates in beautiful simplicity the thought permeating this chapter.

"All I really need to know about how to live and what to do and how to be I learned in kindergarten . . . in the sandpile at Sunday School. These are the things I learned:

Share everything.

Play fair.

Don't hit people

Put things back where you found them.

Clean up your own mess.

19

Patrick J. Brennan

Don't take things that aren't yours.
Say you're sorry when you hurt somebody.
Wash your hands before you eat.
Flush.
Warm cookies and cold milk are good for you.
Live a balanced life — learn some and think some
and draw and paint and sing and dance and plan
and work everyday some.
Take a nap every afternoon.
When you go out into the world, watch out for
traffic, hold hands and stick together.
Be aware of wonder . . . remember Dick and Jane
books and the first word you learned — the biggest word of all — LOOK.

Introduction to Spiritual Exercises

Every chapter of his book concludes with discussion
questions. One approach is to focus on the questions
as an individual. Individuals using the book are encouraged to journal on the questions. Journaling is a
kind of spiritual diary. It might be good to compile
all your attempts at journaling. After completing this
book it would prove interesting to note the change in
mood, feeling and direction taking place in you over
the course of reading. The journal technique is suggested to help you on the spiritual journey and to help
you personalize and put into action some of the themes
and topics.

Others can choose to use the questions as a
springboard for small group sharing. A pastoral-

theological assumption I have is that the Church is renewed when small communities gather to comfort and challenge each other with the wisdom of Jesus.

Journal Questions For Individuals and Small Groups

1) Name some of the people who push power and aggression buttons in you. When and how could you pray more effectively daily, to become more gentle with them?

2) (For another time, after dealing with question one) have prayer and attention made you more gentle in some of your encounters? Has your gentleness provoked gentleness in others? Be specific in your answering and writing.

3) Recall stories of when you used power to achieve a goal, or stories of when it was used on you. How does power and aggression make people feel?

4) What personal price would you/we have to pay to live the message of Matthew 5: 38-48 and this chapter.

5) Name specific people you hope to relate to in a renewed way in the immediate future?

Chapter Two

Get Up: A Reflection on Resurrection

"... The angel spoke addressing the woman: "Do not be frightened. I know you are looking for Jesus the crucified, but he is not here. He has been raised exactly as he promised. Come and see the place where he was laid. Then go quickly and tell his disciples . . ."
Matthew 28: 5-7.

Teaching Seventh Graders

A BIG part of the early years of my priesthood was spent working with youth — junior high, high school, and young adult age people. One aspect of youth ministry that I particularly enjoyed was serving as a catechist to youth. I made it my business to teach religion in the parochial school weekly, and in the School of Religion (CCD) as often as possible. One Wednesday morning I was conducting what I felt to be a profound seventh-grade religion class when I noticed one of the students, Rich, was being particularly disruptive. Then I was a bit heavy handed as a disciplinarian. I called on him, reprimanded him, and told him to get with the flow of the class. Rich went home and told his mother, Marie, that he did not like me, that I was mean.

I mentioned part of Rich's story before in a book,

PASCHAL JOURNEY

The Purple Rainbow. The following Saturday, Rich was on his bicycle, riding against traffic on a very busy street. As young boys do when they want to accelerate, he stood up on the peddles of his bicycle. With head down against the wind, he began to move forward. For a moment, he was not watching what was ahead of him. He ran head on into a van, traveling at thirty-five miles per hour.

I reached the hospital within moments. The doctors, however, had already declared Rich brain dead. They were trying to convince the parents to withdraw extraordinary treatment, so that Rich's young, healthy organs could be given to another. The parents declined. They never gave up hope that their son would recover. However, four or five days into our vigil, as I looked at the heart monitor, young Rich's heart just gave out — stopped. Rich died.

Rich's father and Marie, his mother, live in Delaware now. Marie called me recently to say hello. As usual our conversation turned toward Rich, and those painful days of vigil, then death, then grief. Marie told me some of the story that I had never heard.

A Message on Roller Skates

A few days before his death, Rich had asked his parents to take him to a special village roller skating party. They agreed. While there, a call was issued for a special "couples" round of skating. Rich Jr. asked the mother to be "his date," and skate with him. Marie confessed on the phone to be a real "klutz," totally uncoordinated. Nonetheless, she relented, and skated with her son. In the whirlwind and traffic of young, fast skaters, Marie lost her courage, and balance. She fell. But she not only fell, she says she "crashed" to the floor — to the point of feeling she broke something; felt nauseous, in great pain, and faint. She said she was literally seeing stars, when she saw and heard her seventh grader admonishing her. It was not that he did not care about his mother. It was rather that he was into preteen concern about appearance and what other people were thinking. Developmentally, Rich was into *appearance*. And so, he said: "Ma — get up!. . . Get up Ma. . .Ma.a.. a..a! Get up!"

Marie, not knowing how or if she could, got up — for her son. She slowly ambled — on wheels — to the side. It turned out she had done some damage to one of her knees. But for Rich — the son she little knew would be unconscious and then dead within days, she found the power and strength to get up.

Reflected in a Mirror

Marie continued her story on the phone. Weeks and months after the funeral, she found herself in the bathroom one day, staring in the mirror. She was in a period wherein she wondered how she would make it through a given day, today, let alone the days, weeks and months ahead. She says she stared into the bathroom mirror. She saw a young woman, in her thirties, who had aged rapidly, whose face wore the countenance of loss and depression. Then, she heard in her imagination, the voice of her son from not so long ago. The voice said:

"Ma, get up. Get up Ma . . . Ma . . . a . a . . a . . get up!"

Marie says that the bathroom mirror provided her with a religious experience that day. She decided there, with the help of God and in memory of her son, that she would no longer allow herself to decline in mental, spiritual, or physical health. She decided, with God's help, to get up from depression and the paralysis that loss had induced in her. She subsequently sought the support of friends, and a spiritual guide; she became involved in helping young people her son's age. She literally, consciously began anew.

Now as she talks of her son, she no longer speaks of him in the past tense. She speaks of the ongoing scar in her life that Rich's death was and is. She is forever wounded because of his death. But she also says she talks with him, kids with him, prays through him daily. She experiences him now as a very real, living, spiritual presence.

Resurrection

Marie knows what the paschal (passage) mystery is about; she understands what resurrection is. She has experienced her own personal spiritual resurrection, moving from a kind of emotional - relational death to new life. She also has experienced the resurrection of her son. His physical absence has become for her a real presence. In both the case of Rich and also his mother, through the experience, they remained essen-

25

tially the same; but they also became different as they were transformed.

The Easter Mystery as Approach-Avoidance

I heard of how a growing young parish celebrates Easter. They celebrate an Easter liturgy which sticks to the rubics of the sacramentary fairly faithfully. But to better appeal to their young, affluent community, they also have horse drawn carriages circling the Church, and songs from the movie *Easter Parade,* with Judy Garland, electronically amplified outside for the neighborhood to hear.

Very cute — I suppose! But maybe that style of celebrating Easter is also an attempt to dilute what Easter, or the center of our faith is most about: a cross (struggle, suffering), and an empty tomb (struggle and suffering) were conquered by the power of God. Jesuit educator William O'Malley, thinks that such attempts as the "Easter Parade Easter" are indeed dilutions of the core of our faith. In effect says O'Malley, poorly catechized Catholics have created a kind of "Brand X religion" with its own curious form of Creed. The Creed would sound something like this, O'Malley says (I paraphrase):

I sort of believe in God who started everything . . . but is . . . somewhere out there . . . too busy to communicate with me . . . I sort of believe in Jesus his Son, who taught us to be nice, especially to friends. I believe he was crucified, died, and was buried

. . . which does not make a lot of difference to me since death is a long way off for me . . . they say he rose from the dead, which may or may not be true and ascended into heaven, which again is not a big concern of mine because death is a long way off for me. I believe in the Holy Spirit which is another word for the love we all have for each other . . . I do not want to be called Catholic . . . Christian is better, since you are not tied down by a lot of rules . . . I want to have my kids baptized, and a big Church funeral for me, however. I believe in life everlasting, which again is not a big concern of mine, because death is a long way off. Amen.

The cross/death dimension of the paschal mystery is something most people do not want to face. It is a long way off we say to ourselves. But Rich was thirteen, and his parents in their mid-thirties when Good Friday visited their home.

Here is the core of the Easter mystery that we do not like to face: suffering and death someday are inevitable. But hear the total Good News:

- Jesus died. But the Father said to him on his cross, in his tomb, "get up!" And Jesus did — not the same, but rather tranformed, glorified.
- And Rich died, indeed. But as his heart stopped, the Risen Christ said to him "get up," and he did — a glorified spirit.

- And with the boy's death, his parents died psychologically, emotionally. But Jesus, through their son's voice, said "Get up!" Very dramatically, Marie did — in of all places, her bathroom.
- And Jesus has said to all whom we have loved who have died "Get up." And I believe they have — to eternal life.
- And now Jesus is saying to all of us who suffer, "get up" and we can, if we cooperate with the Holy Spirit.
- And he will say to all of us when we physically die "get up"; and through his power, we can and will.

The core of the Easter mystery is this:
- God can pull life out of death.
- Life is passage — like in nature, through death and struggle to new life.
- Nothing is impossible with God.

God is probably saying "get up" to someone reading this, and going through a struggle period — right now!

The Resurrection of Christ and
the Hubble Telescope

At this writing, the Hubble telescope is getting much attention. Though there are numerous structural flaws in it, it had been hoped that it would eventually be in a position in outer space where it could photograph and send back to earth pictures of the farthest frontiers of the cosmos. The curious thing about light as it descends to earth is that it has already happened some time ago. The sun that we see and feel during the day takes eight minutes to arrive on earth. Similarly, some of the stars that we see at night are transmitting light from gallacular explosions, some from billions of years ago. The light we experience in the present is coming to us from a past event. If things ever get straightened out with the Hubble telescope, we may get photographs from one of the primary creative explosions of the universe — pictures from the very dawn of our universe, more than fifteen billion years ago. Light from that long ago is still reaching us!

Reflecting on the universe and its light helps me get a feeling about resurrection. The resurrection of Christ and the resurrection that we experience in a process way during our days on earth are a bit like the stars/ telescope phenomenon. Almost 2,000 years ago, through the power of God, Jesus was victorious over sin and death. The light of that one event is still coming to and having impact on us today. The light of the first Easter event is carrying the Richs who die to eternal glory. The same light is assuring the Maries left here that our loved ones who have died are with God forever; and we will be someday too. The same Easter light is offering support to the Marie's of the world in their, our struggles *here.* The Risen Christ, in an ongoing way, is saying to her, you, me "Get up; become new!"

Tears, Smiles, and Conviction

I saw some old friends of mine recently. I had not seen them in some time. He, a man in his early senior years, has been diagnosed as having inoperable cancer. Simultaneously, his daughter contracted an even more rapidly spreading form of cancer. I spent some time, after seeing the gentleman, with his wife, and one of his sons, a man about my age, and the latter's wife. They all spoke of the inevitability of their older loved one's death, how they were making plans with him already about what in the wake service and funeral could best express and celebrate his life and faith. But all three in conversation expressed the extra heart-wrenching experience of seeing a young daughter, sister, and sister-in-law, herself with husband and children, going through a similar agony, apparently so prematurely. As our time with each other closed, I said good-bye to each of the three personally. When I came to the son, my peer, I noticed tears welling up in his eyes, streaming down his cheeks, but — he also had a big smile on his face. He grabbed my hand, and shook it with feeling and conviction. Easter was only a couple weeks away. "Happy Easter, Father Brennan!" the man said.

I could not help but stare at him for a moment, at the paradoxical juxtaposition of tears, laughter, conviction, and the words "Happy Easter." I stared because I knew intuitively this man and his family were indeed in agony, but also convinced of the rock bottom of our faith: *Resurrection*.

Go Quickly and Tell

The angel's admonition to go and tell others of the reality of the resurrection is timely for our own day. We reflected already on William O'Malley's notion of Brand X religion and its diluted creed. So many baptized people as well as non-baptized have been poorly evangelized, and have no real feel for and grasp of the power, the life-changing power of the reality of resurrection — Christ's and ours. Whether through verbal or behavioral witness, we who have experienced the empty tomb need to get the message out quickly to anyone whom we know is in the midst of a life struggle, or confronting sin, suffering, or death in any of its forms. Without the good news of the paschal mystery, so many, too many, people are caving in to self-destruction and hopelessness.

Journal Questions for Individuals and Small Groups

1) Try to get 15 - 20 minutes alone and in total silence. Use whatever environment aids in meditation, contemplation for you, e.g., alone in a room in silence or listening to quiet music, walking or walking through nature. Ponder the following: what have

been the death and resurrection journeys in your life to this point. As you reflect on each of these processes, offer praise and thanks to God.

2) To the degree you are comfortable, share with someone or others a time in your life when the paschal mystery was real and tangible.

3) What are some of the factors that contribute toward some people experiencing resurrection in the midst of difficulty, and others falling into despair?

4) The chapter says that many of the baptized and non-baptized have little feeling for the power of the resurrection in their lives. Why are so many people in such a situation? How could we, as believers, change and improve this?

Chapter Three

Now: The Precious Present

*". . . Could you not stay awake for even an hour . . .
the spirit is willing but nature is weak . . ." (Mark 14:
37-38)*

False Alarms

THE past year had been a series of emergency trips
to the hospital for John. His octogenarian mother's
health was failing. Sometimes the presenting symptoms had to do with the heart, other times the kidneys,
or sometimes the lungs. But so often in the past year,
it seemed like this was it! But Catherine, his mother,
had a remarkable resiliency and will to live; and she
always bounced back.

Her situation became more acutely critical recently,
and life support, extraordinary means were called for.
John has taken some criticism from friends and extended family. Their response to the situation has
been: "She has had a long, good life. Let her go. Don't
take extraordinary means to save or extend her life."
John has not been able to have such an easy, facile
approach. With each new crisis, crying out for a life
support decision, he has gone to his mother — explained the situation, asked how she was feeling, and
also solicited her advice and direction. His mother has

always replied, though an invalid, in obvious pain and suffering, "I've never been happier in my life."

She was not ready to leave. Neither was John, who would order the necessary treatment. He was not ready to let her go. He treasured each day and moment he had left with her.

The Real Thing and The Picture

One day not too long ago, John's mother decided, with God, it *was* time to go home to God. I believe quite often older, sick people decide when to stop trying, to let go, to surrender to the dying process. As her vital signs seriously deteriorated, her family was called to her bedside. With children, grandchildren, and great grandchildren coaxing her on to the other side of death, John's mother died.

The day of the funeral, before they closed it, John approached his mother's casket and grasped a picture of her that had been placed there. He held his mother's picture to his chest and hugged it. He hugged it with with such intensity that he seemed to be embracing the more than fifty years of precious moments that he had with her.

The Precious Present Moment

I admire John's relationship with and treatment of his mother a great deal. Throughout the dying process, he seemed to treasure every present moment. His embracing of the picture was a ritual of that. Witnessing his patient, plodding, ever present style, I was struck as to how I — and others — often miss the richness of people and experience in our present moment. We are either longing for the past, or racing toward the future. Rarely do many of us embrace *the now.*

My two rooms in the rectory where I live are a literal mess. They are filled with memorabilia from the past. There's an end table that dates back to the '40s and my parents' first apartment. There's an old radio my brother gave me before he left for the Marines during the Viet Nam War era of the late sixties. It still works! There's an old T.V. that my folks gave me back in 1975. It still works! Bunches of artifacts, books, letters, cards, statues from three parishes where I served line book shelves and cabinets also given to me by parishioners, past and present. I am a man long on sentiment and nostalgia. I do not throw anything away.

In sharp contrast to the artifacts of the past are the symbols of the future in my room, or symbols of where I am headed next. There are three or four small suitcases and overnight bags, that recently I have ceased to store or put away after usage. They are always there, ready to take me to the next town, the next convention, the next diocese, the next mission; institute, or course. Some say the neurotic personality type is an intense prophetic type that feels deeply the sins and mistakes of the age. I like that definition of neurosis and find it easier to accept than many explanations of neurosis in medical — sick terms. I often feel that

Patrick J. Brennan

I am *neurotically prophetic* in that I am a man with a *past,* and a *future,* but also someone who often is missing the present.

The precious present moment — with our parents, our children, our spouse, our friends, with ourselves, with God — so often it is missed. Years later it will crop up as nostalgia for the past or remorse or guilt for opportunities missed. Years later it will be perceived as something missed because we were running; but the dismal disappointment that will be exposed is that we were running in place, running toward a future of empty promises, not equal to the richness we missed in the present moment.

Missing Persons

Perhaps the most horrifying news that we hear on the news, read about in the papers, or see glued on the sides of toll booths are those of people who have disappeared into thin air. The diabolical tone of someone slipping into thin air frightens us. Yet daily we are "missing" people, missing each other, in a way missing ourselves.

Practicing presence is a key piece of and skill for living the Reign of God. The very word *practicing* indicates that we have been mass-socialized to be nonpresent, not attentive to ourselves, others, and God. The most frightening of thoughts is that really no one is depriving us of the present moment and the people that populate, enrich it, but ourselves. Our own in-

PASCHAL JOURNEY

attentiveness, our own retreating to the past or running ahead to the future are doing this.

Practicing Presence: Congruency

Carl Rogers, noted psychologist and educator, has for years advocated that those in the helping professions become congruent with themselves. Congruency refers to *self-awareness*. Part of being a person fully involved in the present involves each of us struggling to be congruent with ourselves. Popular psychological writer Eugene Gendlin has developed Rogers's value as a skill. He calls it the ability to do "focusing." Congruency or focusing — whichever you prefer — involves increasing attempts to name what is going on inside each of us. A lack of congruency or focusing is a serious deficit in practicing presence and embracing the present.

A client in therapy recently said to me: "I feel angry, jealous, hurt, and fearful." I was amazed at his congruency, or focusing ability. As a trained listener, I had heard these four dominant emotional themes swilling around through his story. I was pleased that he was able to name his interior dynamics so clearly. Rollo May (*The Meaning of Anxiety, Love and Will, The Courage to Create,* etc.) has said that feelings within us that go un-named and unfocused upon, go on to become almost demonic forces that control us.

In a similar vein, I was impressed with an octogenarian widower, who recently admitted to me that he was jealous that he did not have a partner in the present to share his life with, as others do in his senior citizen complex. As long as that senior can stay congruent with that feeling, name it, talk about it, he will manage well.

As a therapist and spiritual director, I have often encouraged congruency and focusing as key to an effective, living prayer life. Prayer, at root is the experience of the core of ourselves — experiencing communion with others and with the heart of God.

Practicing Presence: Contemplation as Listening

Contemplation has long scared most of us mundane, busy folks off as rarified stuff practiced by Thomas Merton and the like. Merton biographers document he himself had great struggles with the contemplative life. Recent theories of contemplation are reinterpreting the contemplative spirit as one which is capable of, indeed practices, *listening*.

Listening admits of a number of connotations.

Contemplative listening can be prayerful congruency with, or focusing on, the internal self, as we discussed previously, and lifting up that material in prayerful communication to God. But contemplative listening can also be a disciplined attempt to really attend to the stories and feelings that we hear coming from others. Contemplation means also that we take what we have heard and remembered to the Lord

PASCHAL JOURNEY

in prayer. Contemplation is listening. The contemplative life necessitates a discipline of silence and listening, being one with what or whom we have heard, and — with others and the world now incarnated in us through listening — becoming one, a community, all of us, with the listening God.

Contemplative listening is also a discipline of listening to and reflecting on the world. The Reign of God is a new creation awaiting us with great groaning. If a new creation is to be, more of us need to listen to our world. As Karl Barth pointed out years ago, reading (watching now) the news, is indeed a spiritual activity. The news is stuff we need to listen to, ponder, reflect on, converse with God about, discuss among ourselves, and possibly act on.

Maybe one has to be over forty to be mind-boggled by the events in the recent past in Eastern Europe and the Soviet Union. Changes that we thought to be centuries off happened in a matter of weeks, as Poland, Romania, and Czechoslovakia moved toward becoming democratic nations after forty years of Communist rule. The Berlin Wall came down in days. Now the former Soviet Union is a non-Communist Commonwealth of Independent States. This last issue especially demands prayer and reflection. While the movement of those states toward independence is without doubt the moral course of action, nonetheless the threat of the Soviet Union breaking into Civil War, a super-power with a tremendous nuclear arsenal is a

39

terribly frightening possibility. The threat of a new despotic figure toppling Mikhail Gorbachev from power is a disturbing possibility.

None of those things, and others from the third world, should or can escape our attention, concern, prayer and possible action. Thomas Groome in his classic *Christian Religious Education,* describes the Kingdom of God as "redeemed people trying to redeem society." He goes on to describe religious education as a process of formation that leads to political action, the transformation of society.

Contemplation is being present enough to listen to our loved ones and our world, that is, the movements of the Holy Spirit in our relationships and world.

Practicing Presence: Intimacy

A man told me recently that his line of work had led him to do so many things at one time, that when he returned home he found himself not maintaining eye contact with his wife and children. His learned "buckshot attention span," an acquired skill for the job had become an obstacle to effective communication in his primary relationships.

I could identify with the man's struggle. Early on in ministry I found the temptation to attend to everyone after a liturgy on weekends prevented me from focusing in on the one, small, big, crying, laughing, thin, heavy, pleasant, unpleasant person before me. I have made it a part of my prayer and a spiritual discipline to practice attending to only one person at

40

a time after liturgy. It is easy to campaign in a popularity contest. It is difficult to act "as if" the person with whom you are communicating or speaking is the only person in the world right now.

Intimacy in a relationship is one of the chief fruits of practicing presence and living in the present. Eric Fromm said years ago that it did not really matter whether people were sharing anger or love — what matters is when people really try to share with each other from the core of their being — *from* core *to* core. Intimacy may or may not involve genital sexual expression. I personally feel the "sexiest couples" I see are couples who hold hands shamelessly and seem to express unconsciously a deep quality of communication and intimacy.

Many people, married and single, are too "past" and/or "future" to be "present" enough for communication and intimacy. "All the lonely people," the Beatles asked long ago, "where do they all come from?" Most are racing to success or busyness — or some place.

Practicing Presence: Confronting the Busyness Addiction

Perhaps no characteristic is more uniformly shared in contemporary society than busyness. Everyone seems too busy to be present. Even people like pastors and counselors who were trained to be present have appointment books that mitigate against presence. I was struck recently by a lecture that I attended given

Patrick J. Brennan

by Diane Fassel, an associate of Ann Wilson Schaef, both of whom are experts in substance and process addictions. The latter refers to continuing with compulsive activity that is neither productive nor life-giving. With that definition as a springboard, Fassel went on to describe the basic American addiction as that of "busyness." Fassel described what the busyness addiction does to and for people. It creates a situation of "no room." "No room" refers to *no time* or *no space* for creativity. I have always prized creativity. Thus, Fassel's words cut deeply. Before she spoke, I had been feeling "filled" with commitments, appointments, responsibilities, and expectations. She held up a mirror to me, a reflection of what in fact I was doing to myself, what many of us do to ourselves. We crowd our lives so much that there is no room; and with no room, creativity, often one of the signs of the Spirit working in us, is stifled.

"No room" stifles the discovery that Brother Roger, founder of the Taize community, had forty years ago: "Christ Jesus, following you is discovering this gospel reality: you are praying within each one of us."

I Am

In Scripture, whether Yahweh in the Old Testament, or Jesus in the New Testament, the words "I am" are used to name and describe God. "I am" suggests that while Christ is indeed the Alpha and Omega, the beginning and the end, past and future, he is essentially a God of the present and presence.

PASCHAL JOURNEY

So let us not dwell so much in the past — in guilt, remorse, or revenge, or the future — in worry, fear, control, or apprehension. In so doing, we may very well miss "I am."

Journal Questions for Individuals and Small Groups

1) One type of spiritual growth exercise is called "positive imaging." It involves the uses of the imagination. Open your hands, and using your imagination, place one person, place, or thing from your present life circumstances in your hands. Spend some time listening to, observing, reflecting on, being one with that person, place, or thing.

   After an appropriate time, speak to the Lord in your own words about this person, place or thing. Be present to God with your object of focus.

2) In what ways do you feel *no room,* or creativity blocked in your life?

3) Practicing Presence involves a willingness to work on congruency, contemplative listening, intimacy, and creativity. Which of these are areas that strike you as areas of special need in your life?

4) How does the past and future keep us from being present?

Chapter Four

Hope: Holding On Through Life's Turnings

"... Our Lord Jesus Christ ... gave us new birth; a birth unto hope which draws its life from the resurrection of Jesus Christ from the dead. ... There is cause for rejoicing here. You may for a time have to suffer the distress of many trials ... but this is so your faith ... may lead to promise, glory, and honor when Jesus Christ appears (1 Peter: 1: 3-7).

I HAVE worn a lot of hats during my years of ordained ministry: parish priest, youth minister, graduate school professor, director of both local and national organizations for evangelization and spiritual renewal, and both a pastoral counselor and a practicing psychotherapist. In the midst of all of this I have had the privilege of standing with people in the midst of struggle and pain.

Life's Surprises

Vivid in memory are stories of parents who experienced the unexpected, premature death of a child, teenager, or young adult. What, in such a great experience of loss, could ever sustain parents or a family through such pain? Vivid also are stories of people coming to grips with addiction in their lives: some troubled by alcohol, others by drugs, still others by food or gambling or some other compulsion. What has facilitated liberation in their lives? Others have known the loss of a loved one: either through abandonment, or divorce, or death. What helps a person to hold on when he or she has lost hold or touch with someone beloved? There has been suicide, and the broken lives of those left behind. There were and are victims of physical and sexual abuse, living, but living with scars.

I personally believe joy is greater than pain in life. But I am a realist enough to say that the stories and examples that I have lived with are not the stuff of soap operas. They are struggle experiences that are part of people whose lives in some way have merged with mine. In fact, maybe some of you have experienced some of the painful situations that I mentioned or others that I have not mentioned.

Life's Age and Stage Transitions

Besides these "life accident" moments, there are intrinsic to life, other turnings that seem relentlessly to happen to each of us. I am speaking of life stage transitions. Beginning in our twenties and extending throughout the life span, life seems to come unglued for us every seven to ten years. There is the early young adult transition, from adolescence to the early twenties. There are the mid-twenties and the establishment of the first adult life structure, made up of vocation and commitments. But already in the late twenties, a process of re-evaluation has begun that throws people into the chaos of the '30s transition. There's a settling down period that really is the calm before the storm of the '40s transition. The mid-forties are the beginning of mid-life, which extends into the sixties.

Mid-life has gotten the most press or attention in terms of the difficulty that period contains. But, in fact, all the life stage transitions are painful; for in them the ground on which our lives have settled becomes shaken. In all of these transitions, our dreams, self concept, sense of vocation, style of relationships, and sense of life's meaning can change. Our lives can experience growth, regression, or an actual falling apart. A fact that will change American life significantly in the future is the growing number of people surviving and continuing to live well into their eighties and nineties. There are actually at least three sub-eras within old age: the senior years transition, the actual senior years, and the old — old of the 80s' plus group. We are mistaken if we write these people off as not struggling with change as much as the mid life person or young adult. Aging, sickness, the loss of a partner, and other issues are all difficult experiences for one to cope with.

So life is filled with turnings, some of an intrusive nature like life accident moments. Others are more natural parts of the aging process. Why in the face of these experiences do some people seem to "cash in their chips," and if they do not become self destructive, they at least give in to despair? Why do others seem to go on, and not just *go on;* but actually experience profound growth and a greater appreciation of the mystery of life?

Hope

The factor which seems to make the difference between despair and growth is *Hope*. People who grow, or are converted, or are spiritually and emotionally transformed, seem to experience hope, or the ability to hold on or "keep on keeping on." Hope is that quality of life which intuits or sees shafts of life in tunnels of darkness. Hope senses possibilities in the face of dead ends. Hope feels there is purpose or meaning in apparent meaninglessness.

"Hope springs eternal," the saying goes. Well, the first two words *hope springs* almost sound like what hope does for a life. In the midst of life's turnings and transitions, hope is that reality that helps us spring forward or more deeply into life's mysteries. People without hope are like aircraft with their engines in reverse. Hope, rather, is that forward thrust that is so much needed for the aircraft to take off.

Hope as a By-product

But hope really is a by-product of something else: a deep, abiding *conviction* that there is a Loving Someone in the midst of all reality, caring for us, ordering all things for the good of us all. Jesus called this Loving Someone "Father," and taught that the Father was

47

Patrick J. Brennan

active in each of our lives *invisibly* but *really* as the Holy Spirit. A life with hope is the result of a person having personally encountered the Father, Son, and Spirit. The encounter usually results in a *convictional experience* — no matter what: life is good; God is good; new life and learning can always flow from chaos and struggle. In the worldview that I am espousing, God is not the source of pain and difficulty. Rather, as Rabbi Harold Kushner says in *When Bad Things Happen to Good People,* bad things are simply a part of the human story. God is not the agent of bad things, but *rather, hope, help, and healing for the bad times.*

Victor Frankl, in *Man's Search for Meaning* and *Logotherapy* says that our basic hunger is to find amidst life's obstacles and difficulties, a sense of meaning and purpose. Often this sense of meaning and purpose is the birth of hope coming from an encounter with God, someone else's witness to God, or a jump of our intuition or imagination to the hope God can give us. Frankl says if we discover a *why* we can get through anything. Discovery of the *why* helps us to create a *how,* or a strategy for not only survival and coping but also genuine hope.

Hope, meaning, a sense of life's deep purposiveness flow from conversion experiences, *God encounters,* that often one has as a result of life's turnings, life accidents or life stage transitions. Remember, the basic hunger and thirst for meaning and hope are inherent. Lutheran theologian, Martin Marty says, somewhat tongue in cheek, that everyone walking down the street with a copy of Shirley's Maclaine's latest book on re-incarnation is looking for meaning and hope. But the God encounter, or discovery of meaning and hope is something not arrived at easily. Often turnings appear to be voids, darkness, emptiness; and God seems to be absent rather than present. It is so vitally important for people of all ages, to have companionship or mentoring relationships in the midst of life's difficulties. Without quality companioning or mentoring, the potential conversion can easily become *mere breakdown* and not *break-through*.

Mentoring refers to being with another on a deep level, and picking up on that person's vision and values. Conversion, hope, meaning are often the direct result of being with another person of conversion, hope, and meaning. Positive values almost jump from one person to the other.

It is because I am convinced of the importance of reminding each other of God in the mentoring process, that I encourage believers of all ages to *re-imagine* ministry and parish in terms of *a network of small support groups, mentoring communities that meet on a regular basis for prayer, life sharing, Scripture study and some sort of shared ministry.* These groups are being proven internationally as the best means of staying on a conversion journey amidst life's turnings.

The alarming reality is that you and I cannot help but *be mentored.* If we are not, in a sense, shepherding each other in the values of the Kingdom, we will be mentored or influenced by the values of American consumerism, which are oriented toward success and individualism, but not the happiness and hope that come from meeting God in conversion.

If you know of someone in a void, go to that person and *"faith"* with him or her; this is true ministry. If you yourself are in a void, do not be so proud as to not seek the mentoring assistance of another person. A new experience of God and life can be awaiting you in one of your life's turnings. But you should not, need not, enter the void alone.

Let us be reminded that we all have a mission because of Baptism: to *shepherd each other in hope* down the winding roads of life's turnings and transitions, toward God, Jesus, the Spirit, God's reign and influence in our lives.

In his book *A Gift of Hope,* Tony Melendez tells the story of how his mother was the mentor figure who imbued in him a sense of hope that he would break through the difficulties of his life. Tony was born without arms, the result of his mother being given a problematic drug during her pregnancy. Despite unbelievable obstacles, Tony learned to play the guitar with his feet and compose and sing beautiful spiritual music. Nonetheless, the jobs were sporadic and the money not much. Tony would grow despondent. But his mother would always shore him up with the words, "Don't worry Tony . . . God has something wonderful in mind for you. Trust God, and don't get impatient."

PASCHAL JOURNEY

Tony says he thought of his mother's hopeful words as he waited to sing for the Pope in Los Angeles—a surprise in his life that he had not expected. After he performed, a young woman, similarly disabled said to him from a wheelchair, "Thank you Tony, you give me hope." She was re-echoing the words of John Paul II who said to Tony after one of his songs: "You are giving hope to all of us." Tony has begun a beautiful life of mentoring thousands toward *hope.*

Tony concludes: "It's a mystery . . . God could use this armless kid from Nicaragua to bring hope . . . God can use me . . . God also can use you . . . If we let him . . . God will use us to bring a little hope . . . into our . . . dying world. . . . Remember what my mother said to me . . . "Don't worry. God has something wonderful in mind for you. Trust God and don't get impatient."

Journal Questions for Individuals and Small Groups

1) Make a list of all the people who have encouraged you throughout life, and how.

2) Make a second list of how *you* may discourage others and how you can turn this negative energy around.

3) Liturgist - composer Rory Cooney has written a song entitled "Do Not Fear to Hope." The title suggests we actually grow afraid to hope. Why might this be?

Patrick J. Brennan

4) Norman Cousins in *Head First: the Biology of Hope* says that hope plays a quite positive role on body chemistry and health. The loss of hope likewise contributes to disease. Do you agree? Tell stories to support your opinion.

5) Name and describe the qualities of someone you know who is hopeful.

Chapter Five

Will: The Reality of the Human Will and Its Implications for Growth

". . . The slave called in the Lord is a freed person, just as the free person who has been called is a slave of Christ . . ." (1Cor. 7:22-23).

Poor Me

ONE OF the easiest cop-outs to pull in life is to take on the role of either the psychological *"victim"* or *"the martyr."* I have written on these syndromes in previous books. Basically, victims stay in bad situations or relationships. They come to a counselor often in pain. They want the pain removed but *cannot, will not* muster up the psychic energy to get to the root of the problem and change. Maybe they even have forgotten, or never learned that they have the ability to change. *Martyrs* are very similar to *victims,* but they find some spiritual or theological reason for not changing—staying the same is equated somehow with spiritual heroics of self sacrifice.

I have found, in trying to help others, and in trying to grow myself, two preliminary things are often needed before growth or change can take place. The first is the person must catch him or herself in an obviously unhealthy tactic, situation, or relationship, and

Patrick J. Brennan

make a decision to change. The second step needed is to harness and focus on an often forgotten, at least not discussed, energy. That energy is the *human will.*

Though I firmly believe, as I will mention later, that sometimes growth is had in spiritual surrender, we too often forget that often what is needed is an *exercise of the will.* We must respect the research that is coming out regarding biochemical contributions to anxiety, depression, and other emotional pain and also the research into genetic predispositions some have toward addictions. In other words, for some people, emotional pain has little to do with their own choices. There is a certain physical — chemical — genetic determinism about their condition. But for many others, suffering from garden variety fears and downers, the issue is that they are not using a God-given ability: the human will. Not using will, they often take on the posture of *"poor me,"* that is, I have no control over the direction of my life.

In this chapter, we will explore the reality of will. Surprisingly, its existence and power have been debated for thousands of years.

The Will Down Through History

Let us begin this analysis of the evolving theory of will with the thought of St. Augustine. It should be noted that Augustine (354 A.D. - 430 A.D.) was indeed a troubled man for a time in his life — unhappy with his own values, direction, and morality. For a while he became part of the Manichean movement, which held that human reason alone could make human beings wise. Gradually he became disillusioned with Manicheism and pursued the Neoplatonic movement, largely being influenced by Plotinus and Porphyry. Augustine later claimed that the Neoplatonists freed his mind of materialism and began to purify his moral life. However, it was even later, during a period of profound spiritual conversion and transformation, that Augustine began to equate wisdom with alliance with Jesus Christ, the Wisdom of God. Augustine felt *Christ* was light to the mind and *strength to the will.*

Augustine, thus, was an early adherent to the concept of *will.* A neo-Platonic adherent to the reality of soul, Augustine divided the faculties of soul into three: memory, understanding, and *will.* Augustine's notion of the will permeates the walls between philosophy, psychology and theology. But he held the *will* to be the most important faculty of the mind. Interestingly, Augustine's emphasis on *the divine as strength for the will* is echoed today in Alcoholics Anonymous, and all twelve-step programs, that speak of addictions as syndromes that break down the strength of will. The weakened, damaged will can only be strengthened with attention to and co-operation with the Higher Power, however one envisions him, her, it. According to Augustine, evil is not something in and of itself, but rather the absence of good. When the human species was created, men and women were given *free will* to do good or not. But through the intersection into the human story of sin, the human race has fallen and in fact has little strength to choose the good, via human resources. "Fallen man" is enslaved to passions and to the sensible world; which distract him from his own soul and God. Augustine felt that people do not will the good, or if they do, they cannot do the good that they will. Thus, human beings require a moral and an intellectual *illumination.* Immutable eternal law has to illuminate human conscience and leave an impression upon it. It is not enough, however, Augustine thought, for conscience to become aware of natural law. *The human will must be rectified* so that it will yield to divine, natural law, and then put it into practice.

The rectification of the will is brought about by the illuminating action of divine virtues. The virtues of prudence, fortitude, temperance, and justice reside in God; they shine upon the soul, like lights, establishing within the world, a moral order. Thus, God becomes the life of the soul, ordering it from within; the soul, in turn, gives life and order to the body.

We will soon take note of Thomas Aquinas's thinking on the will. It is important to note that Augustine was a tremendous influence on early medieval thinking. He built on the philosophy of Plato. The next great mind, to influence later medieval thought would be Thomas Aquinas, who reached back to build his speculative system on Aristotle. Thus, the *two most influential medieval thinkers were influenced by Plato and Aristotle.* Between Augustine and Aquinas there were several lesser lights, who nonetheless were proponents

56

of the reality and influence of *will*. Among them are *Boethius, Anselm, Abelard, Bonaventure, and Albert the Great* — all precursers of Thomas Aquinas.

Again, I find it interesting to note Augustine's conviction about the *powerlessness or depravity of the human will*, and the need for *divine illumination* to rectify the will, and *parallel notions in contemporary twelve-step programs*. Wherever one stands on the reality or non-reality of the deity, there is little doubt of the efficacy of those steps in such programs dedicated to the admission of powerlessness and the need for a higher power intervention.

Boethius, Anselm, Abeland, Bonaventure and Albert the Great

Boethius (born 480 in Italy), wrestled with the tension between *Providence* (*God's will* and plan for all of life and humanity) and *human free will*. He wondered how people can have free will if God foresees and directs all things. Boethius resolved this dilemma with this conclusion: God sees all things in the eternal present, but His knowledge of our freely chosen acts (thus, *Boethius believes in free will*) does not impose necessity on them.

Anselm (an 11th century monk in the post-Charlemagne Empire), followed much of the thinking of St. Augustine. A fierce defender of the faculty of willing, Anselm felt the word *will had three meanings*. It refers *first* to the faculty of willing. A second connotation refers to the *inclination, propensity or affection of the power of will.* The will is inclined to do the useful and the just. These positive inclinations can always be lost through the power of sin. The third connotation of will is the *very act of willing.* The act is the exercise and manifestation of a power. Thus for Anselm, humans were created with free choice, exercised through will, inclined toward the useful and the just. Nonetheless *the will can become misdirected* through evil. Herein humans lose dignity and human freedom. *Misdirected will is in need of the grace of God* for redemption and rectitude. Anselm's pre-occupation with the will was moral and religious rather than psychological.

Peter Abelard's teachings on the will were also ethical and moral in nature, though he tried to present his teachings in a more coherent, scientific style than Boethius or Anselm. Abelard (a 12th century philosopher) saw acts in themselves as morally neutral. An action becomes bad because it springs from a bad intention. Good intentions are those that conform to God's will and intention.

Though Abelard, Anselm and Boethius approached will from a theistic-moral viewpoint, all nonetheless were concerned about what we now recognize to be a *psychological* dynamic, namely *intentionality.* Augustine himself felt that *willing referred to decisions that we make about what we will attend to.* As Augustine's emphasis on divine rectitude of the will is re-echoed in today's 12 step programs, the *"will as intention,"* or *"decisions about what to pay attention to,"* are, in seminal form what Rollo May in *Love and*

PASCHAL JOURNEY

Will, and others would call *intentionality* in describing the functions of will.

In the thirteenth century Bonaventure continued Augustine's thought and its heavy emphasis on the need for illumination of the soul and the will for rectitude and moral intentionality, that is, congruence with God's will.

A pivotal person during this period is someone who has come to be known as Albertus Magnus, or Albert the Great, a German educated as a Dominican in Padua, who died in 1280. Though his philosophy does not have the brilliance of a Thomas Aquinas, his importance lies in his switch from a heavily *Platonic* to an *Aristotelian* base. It was Albert the Great who taught and influenced Thomas Aquinas.

Though greatly influenced by Christian faith, all of the writers touched on so far can be seen to contain in seminal form, strands of thinking that later would become part of 1) *addiction therapy;* 2) *the notion of intentionality in psychotherapy;* and 3) *the heavy emphasis on teleology or meaning and purposefulness in people's behavior in Adlerian thought.* This latter is articulated well in *On Purpose* by Harold Mosak (1977).

Thomas Aquinas

Aquinas (born in Naples in 1225; died in 1274) thought that it was necessary for human beings to have free will to pursue and actualize what is good. Will, for Aquinas was an intellectual appetite; that is, it rises

Patrick J. Brennan

from an intellectually derived notion of good. *Humans use will,* unlike other animals, to control their passions. To summarize Aquinas's thought, human beings have *choice.* For example he taught that a person can shut his or her eyes to the truth and turn attention to merely sensual pleasures. Aquinas's apriori conviction is that the human person is *oriented toward the good,* and the good is always found in conscious communion with God, the divine.

Whether one accepts Aquinas' theistic foundation or not, it is important to notice the precision in his thought. Whatever human beings will, they will as a good — *real or apparent.* The act of will-choice may or may not lead one, consciously or unconsciously, toward something that is *lacking* in happiness, grace, or communion with God. If a conscious choice-action, we move into the area of discerning morality. But if there is some form of ignorance in choosing evil over good, moral culpability is indeed mitigated. Here again we have in seminal form, ideas that will expand in later psychological theory. Alfred Adler's and Rudulf Dreikur's notion of "mistaken notions" in the lifestyle seem to find congruence with some of Aquinas' thought. In the Adlerian view, as pointed out earlier, there is a high degree of teleology — views, convictions, attitudes, behaviors (the vision and the praxis of life) are constructed in pursuit of happiness and belonging, that is, in pursuit of meaning and purpose.

Like Aquinas, Adlerians say that on the level of will and intentionality we are oriented toward good. Yet in the movement toward good, we can decide for mistaken notions that rob us of the very end that we are pursuing. The notions can be *corrected through education*. Aquinas' Scholastic tradition would say the same in its theory of vincible (that is "able — to — be overcome") ignorance.

After Aquinas

The reality or non-reality of will was an object of fierce debate after Thomas's death. *John Duns Scotus* (born in 1265 in Scotland, died in Cologne in 1308) was a fierce defender of the will. He went so far as to speak of the *primacy of the will* over the intellect. Scotus placed a great emphasis on liberty. In his view, will does not add anything to understanding. Rather the will co-operates mediately, moving the intellect to attend to this or that intelligible object, or to consider arguments. Scotus, like other philosopher — churchmen, went on to speak of will in *heavily moral terms*.

Late Medieval and Renaissance philosophy in Europe was highly influenced by Scholastic (Thomistic) thoughts. It became an age of speculative mysticism. However, during the period of the Reformation, *Martin Luther* and *John Calvin* vigorously *denied the reality of free will*, operating out of a heavy emphasis on the *pre-destination of souls*.

Movements Toward Modern Thought

Baruch Spinoza of Amsterdam, was one of the first thinkers, in the seventeenth century, to begin to

61

minimize or dismiss the importance of will. Spinoza saw self-preservation, not meaning or purpose as the aim of all behavior. With each piece of behavior *determined* by previous actions, *will* is an unneeded concept for Spinoza.

With Thomas Hobbes (1588-1679) we see the beginning of modern philosophy in Britain. *Hobbes believed in the concept of will.* But he saw it as one of many, indeed the last, appetite that is operative in the bigger process of deliberation. Because animals also deliberate, Hobbes felt animals possessed the appetite of will also.

John Locke (1642-1704) George Berkeley (1685-1753) and David Hume (1711-1776) mark the beginning of what has become known as the British empirical movement. Hume especially spoke of will as *just another observable feeling* that we are in control of, either through bodily movement or intellectual operations. In the *Enquiry Toward Human Understanding,* Hume described will as the internal impression we feel and are conscious of when we knowingly give rise to any new motion of our body, or new perception of our mind.

Thomas Reid, a Scot, (1710-1796) was among those that countered the *skeptical, reductionistic views* of the early empiricists, *defending the will* as one of the active powers of the mind. James Mill (18th century) was influenced by German thinkers in dividing the functions of the mind into knowing, feeling, and willing. His thought was developed by his son John Stuart

Mill. They explained will through associationist principles: what is willed or not willed is intimately connected, associated to experiences, feelings of pleasure or pain.

Kant

Immanuel Kant (1724-1804), of both German and Scottish descent, rooted his thinking in German philosophy (e.g., Gottfried Leibniz [1646-1716]). Chief among Kant's theories was that of the *categorical imperative*. By this term, Kant meant that all rational beings *ought* to act in a certain way. They ought to act on those maxims which they can, *will*, without contradiction, to be *universal laws*. Kant's thinking gets increasingly complicated as he tried to hold in balance the universal moral imperatives that *the will intuits* and must act on, and the concept of *human freedom* which he also espoused.

Wilhelm Wundt and William James

Especially with Wundt, we see psychology branching off, away from philosophy to indeed become a science on its own. *Wundt considered will or volition to be a basic function of psychic functioning,* in opposition to the associationist principles referred to previously. He postulated that will could be *experimentally demonstrated.* Wundt's voluntarism, in fact, gave birth to American motivational research. Later researchers after Wundt would divide will into both a *formal principle,* and *its effects: the will to learn,*

Patrick J. Brennan

to live, to achieve, to value, etc. Pioneers of motivational theory became convinced that genuine volitional motives are conscious, or that hidden motives can be made conscious in an act of recall.

Ach (1905) and other early experimental psychologists, through experiments, showed that the concept of *will refers to a special energy potential,* which is able to overcome strong contrary forces — especially forces like association — oriented inhibitions. In Ach's research and experiments he found that *a will-motivational act* leads to a *decision,* which leads to *goal-setting,* and then the *taking of action.* The *energy force of will* keeps one intent on the goal for long periods of time.

Adler's research was congruent with Ach's. Again, Adler discovered that *a deficit in will was something learned,* and *the person was able to be re-educated.*

Some psychologists down through the years have actually postulated and experimented around the notion of will as *genuine kinetic energy,* an impelling and affective force. Others have more recently studied the will as an energy force that can be oriented inward or outward, and, at root, the *font of decision making.*

Like Wundt, William James (1842-1910) was *antireductionistic* or *minimalistic* when it came to *will.* He felt that the functions of the mind and personality could not be understood without taking the will into consideration. Critiquing associationism in his *Varieties of Religious Experience,* James wrote concerning the will: "Let us hereafter, in speaking of the hot place in man's consciousness, the group of ideas to which he devotes himself, and from which he works, call it the habitual center of his energy." For James, *willing* is not mere *wishing*. Not the superficial wish but the deep — seated *will* is a strong expression of the self. James felt will had much to do with *life changing* or *life-sustaining choices.* He felt its development came largely through *struggle and fragility* — in his own case, dealing with free floating anxiety.

Present Implications for Growth, Counseling, and Psychotherapy

This survey of thought regarding the will is important for my purposes as a psychotherapist in the light it brings to current therapeutic insights and practices.

1) I have already mentioned the connection between Augustine and the post-Augustinian writers, their emphasis on the will needing rectitude or discipline, and the praxis of twelve-step programs that stresses the admission of *acquired* powerlessness, moral decline, and the need for a higher power to *heal broken will.*

2) The heavy moralistic grounding of much pre-Freudian thought must be viewed in the context of the religious age in which it was developed. Whether talking the *language of sin or sickness,* the role of the will in wholistic living or

Patrick J. Brennan

disintegration is high-lighted in these early writings, and I have found evidence of it in the counselling office.

3) The *Aristotelian-Thomistic* and *post-Thomistic scholastic emphasis on the will seeking an end* (the good, God) *is a precursor of the highly teleological Adlerian concept of the lifestyle.* A misguided will that misses the mark is likewise a seminal version of Adler's notion of therapy as re-educating mistaken notions and misguided goals.

4) In the early thinkers as well as in Wundt and James, we hear hints of May's (1969) concept of neurosis as *misguided intentionality,* and therapy as helping one gain healthy intentionality.

5) The importance of will is clearly stated in the Adlerian emphasis on the need for *courage* in attempting to grow in therapy, and similar theories espoused by May (1975) in *The Courage To Create.*

6) Will has been highlighted as vital in therapeutic processes involving anxiety, phobias, and depression in the more recent works of: a) Victor Frankl (1973, 1978), and his technique of paradoxial intention, wherein one wills a painful emotional symptom to occur, thus, robbing it of its power; b) Dr. Gerald May (1982) and his blending of willfulness (intentionality) and willingness (sur-

66

render) in therapeutic growth; c) and the will to discomfort needed for true growth, spoken of by Dr. Bernard Tyrell in his pastoral psychotherapy, and in his books *Christotherapy I & II*.

7) I myself have discovered that successful therapy involves helping a client to: a) *gain insight;* b) *make decisions;* c) *set goals;* d) *attempt change.* But the *energy* to move from (a) to (d) lies in the *reservoir of will.* Will is intimately connected with the *dynamics of hope* needed in any therapeutic process. I wrote of this in my book, *The Purple Rainbow,* and in a previous chapter of this book.

Perhaps we are living in *another age that is minimizing the importance and power of will.* The narcissism, immediate gratification, and lack of commitment evidenced in consumer society and commented on by Allen Bloom in *The Closing of the American Mind* and others, has ushered in also a concommitant *nihilism and hopelessness,* frequently evidenced in the deterioration of family life, self-destruction, and substance abuse.

Journal Questions for Individuals and Small Groups

1) Dr. Gerald May in his book *Will and Spirit* says a growing person needs to discern when to be *willful* (self-determining and intentional) and when to be *willing* (living in a posture of spiritual surrender).

Patrick J. Brennan

Comment on those areas of your life where you need to become more *willful* and *willing.*

2) This chapter said psychologist William James had to wrestle with his own anxieties and depression to fully discover the power and importance of his own will. Did you (or anyone else in the group) have such an experience? Tell stories about such self discoveries.

3) Christopher Lasch, in his book, *The Culture of Narcissison* describes Western Culture as increasingly self-preoccupied. Where do you or your group see narcissism or preoccupation with self — acutualization getting in the way of life tasks like intimacy, friendship, generativity, etc.?

4) In trying to direct one's will toward health and growth, how does one know whether he/she is doing God's will?

Chapter Six

Innocence: On Being Child-Like

"... Let the little children come to me. ... Do nothing to stop them. ... It is to just such as these that the Kingdom of God belongs. I assure you: unless you become like a little child you will never enter the Kingdom. ... Then He embraced them, placed His hands on them and blessed them ..." Mark 10:14-16.

A First Communion

I RECENTLY had the privilege of witnessing over one hundred third graders celebrate their first communion. My principal focus at the celebration was my niece, Heather, who was celebrating her first communion. The white dress, well-rehearsed songs, gestures with the songs, and the steeple-like folded hands radiated reverence, devotion and innocence. Perhaps "you are what you wear" or something like that was operative here, because Heather's demeanor at her First Communion was almost antithetical to what we have been experiencing lately.

My niece is only nine years old; yet already things have begun to become tough in relating to her. She is argumentative with her mother about the use of make-up and earrings. Unlike many of us, who at the same age, wore generic clothes or hand-me-downs,

Patrick J. Brennan

designer clothes are a *must* for this little girl. I thought she was an exception until I mentioned some of our struggles with her recently in a homily, and a number of mothers approached me relating similar struggles with their children, who would only wear the best of *Nike* or *Reebok* shoes. Later, I heard a woman on the radio confess to feeling almost held hostage to her children's demands for a certain kind of pre-teen, designer clothing.

Heather is worried about "cool" already. That concern did not hit me until well into my teens. I have my doubts as to whether I ever met the criteria for being cool. But what concerns me is that such young people, little children that I know and love, are preoccupied with it as an issue.

"Where is all this coming from?" my brother asked, after a recent parent-teacher conference at which my niece was critiqued for some behavioral problems. I wished I had an easy, facile answer for him. The fact is any child's acting out can come from a cluster of causes, integrating internal family, peer group, and cultural dynamics. But I would like to *underscore the dominant* culture as the most insidious yet potent source of negative influence on our children. American culture has become corrupt, and is corrupting the innocence of our young people.

Culture . . . and culture

In referring to "the culture," it is easy to over generalize and speak of the world around us as "the big bad wolf." It is important to nuance the notion of culture. America has been over the years too much of a melting pot, boiling down peoples' customs and nationalities' traditions into a tepid soup of assimilation and conformity. In fact, we have all come from some *racial ethnic rootedness* that ought not to be paved over, but rather named, affirmed, and celebrated. For example, the Irish, the Poles, the Italians, the Germans, the Slavs, and others, who were the backbone of Industrial Revolution America, came with customs and traditions that were good and beautiful and on which faith traditions were built.

Similarly new immigrants to America are coming with cultures. These ought not to be subject to assimilation. Rather we ought to allow the gospel to sink root in them, and create ever new, beautiful, unique experiences of Christianity and Catholicism. Technically, this is called in pastoral theology and ministry, "inculturation." It is because the Catholic Church and mainline Protestant churches do not allow this cultural diversity and mutual enrichment between Gospel and culture to exist, that we/they are losing many believers to the newer, evangelical style churches.

But inculturation and culture in general, have other connotations. Over the last decades, the inter-facing of consumerism and media have produced *"consumer culture."* Consumer culture is an American western-society-type of existence that is increasingly focused on *things, materialism* and *immediate gratification* as

71

Patrick J. Brennan

ends and goals unto themselves.

Consumer culture is a modern term that expresses that ancient truth from Genesis that people have a tendency to choose apples, or things, over people. So, the pursuit of "the mythical it," as Theodore Issac Rubin puts it in his book *Reconciliation: Inner Peace in an Age of Anxiety,* becomes a thankless, meaningless, impossible, always frustrating way of life. Everything else, including relationships, spirituality, and meaning becomes secondary. This is obviously a distortion of the way God intended life to be. Thus, another dimension of inculturation is bringing the gospel to bear down on, to critique in a prophetic way, some of the dehumanizing tendencies of the culture. We need, then, both the inculturation of faith, and the evangelization of dominant, consumer culture.

Relative to gospel values, then, inculturation is both a *birthing process* (the gospel coming to life in the new soil of a given subgroup's approach to life), and a *critiquing process* (calling on the popular culture for those areas in which it has drifted from the gospel.)

The very word *culture,* then, can set off both positive and negative reactions within us. Let us focus for a moment on the more negative connotation of culture, that is the negative values of consumer culture, misshaping us and society, in fact, misshaping the church. Herein lies the answer to my brother's question "where does she get all this?" Heather, like so many young people, and adults as we will discuss later, are very much influenced by what psychologist

PASCHAL JOURNEY

Bruno Bettelheim called the culture's "louder voice."
With great wisdom the 1988 revision of the Rite of Christian Initiation of Adults spoke of "the baptized uncatechized" as a special focus for catechetical efforts. The writers recognized that for many, the waters of baptism have been poured, but, in effect, their souls have become Teflon. Gospel values just have not stuck.

The Influence of TV: An Example

In her insightful book, *The Critical Years,* Sharon Parks states that people cannot help but be *mentored.* Translated? You and I *will* be influenced, swayed, persuaded, guided by some people and forces in life. Erik Erikson in his pioneering work in childhood, adolescent, and young adult developmental psychology, wrote decades ago of how young people, before moving into adulthood, either reach a stage of ideological commitment, or wander in a kind of value confusion. Park's and Erikson's insight have been given credibility by a recent study done by the American Board of Pediatricians. These doctors, who work with such a great focus on the young, say that television watching is definitely having a negative effect on the *imagination,* that is, the dominant values and images of young people. TV is teaching young people that *aggression* is a quick answer to life's problems, and that human *sexuality* is something to be trivialized. The latest research shows that most inner city children have their first experience of intercourse or genital sexuality at around age eleven; most suburban youth have such an experience certainly by age sixteen. The dimension of commitment relative to sexual experience has been almost removed; it is no longer expected. Sexuality has become a trivial pursuit. TV watching also leads, the study says, to *loneliness, depression, feelings of isolation from others and obesity,* as our young pop junk food into their mouths while simultaneously consuming mind candy.

Shepherding

Jesus's recurring reference to himself in John's gospel as the Shepherd, the Good Shepherd, is an articulation of how he (Jesus), his vision and values can become a new source of guidance and mentoring for our young. What remains problematic for me is the huge number of young people who have been baptized, Protestant or Catholic, but for whom Jesus either never was, or is not, a mentoring, shepherding force. However, the shepherding of Jesus toward our young can only be *mediated* through other persons. Specifically, Jesus shepherds, through parents, teachers, and other significant adults in our childrens' lives. Young people often do not meet the Good Shepherd because of a couple of dynamics going on in the lives of their significant adults.

Parents Who Have Lost Control — Lost Sheep Adults

I felt sorry for Karl's mother, Chris. Her fifteen-year-old son is a foul-mouthed, drug abusing kid with a criminal record for theft. Whether at counseling sessions or at home or on the streets, his approach to her is demeaning and abusive. As I have worked with them, I have come to see that perhaps only a "Tough Love, removal from the *house* to another place of residence" answer will work. Chris has lost control, at least temporarily of her son. I do not mean control in a "over-abusing sense." Rather, I mean she has lost the ability to be a positive, authoritative, guiding person in her son's life. The peer group, mass media, the drug culture has taken over. Of course, Karl's dad left him and his mother while Karl was still in the womb. And Karl's two older sisters went on after the divorce to become drug addicted. What positive mentoring has Karl received in this family of origin whose father is absentee, older sisters are addicted, and mother is barely keeping her head above water psychologically? Long before it got to this point, someone should have intervened to serve as what psychologist David Elkind calls "a marker" for this young man.

For Elkind, a marker is an adult who is adult enough to point the way for young people. Asked recently what role the Church should play in family life in the future, Elkind replied that the Church's greatest contribution to families would be to remind parents, or teach them for the first time, how to be markers, guideposts, shepherds for their young.

A second problem in the adult-young person dynamics that is problematic is that so many adults — Catholic, Protestant, or unchurched — have yet to be mentored or shepherded by Christ. Again, it does not matter a lot whether Baptismal water has been poured, if no conversion experience has happened yet. Being led astray by mentoring forces other than Jesus is not just a child's problem. It is certainly a phenomenon that adults share in. Adult sheep are being led by voices that advocate success, achievement, independence, materialism, busyness, racism, sexism, ageism, militarism, power, and others as the keys to happiness. We breathe this stuff in as adults like air pollution, unaware or unconscious of the damage that it is doing. We in turn pass the bad air on, like secondary smoke, to our young people.

Thus, young people not only have the undertow of being negatively mentored by the culture; to the degree they are influenced by adults, they often are being seduced by values that never can provide them with the life meaning and foundation that they need.

How could a parent or adult help these young people that they love? Become a marker, a shepherd, a guide? Yes. *But:* perhaps a preliminary step is to allow one's self to be mentored, influenced by the person and message and ministry of Jesus.

This Generation!

In one of his discourses in Luke's *Acts of the Apostles,* Peter admonishes his listeners not to be swayed by this generation that has gone astray. The image of Peter delivering that strong message jumped onto the screen of my imagination last week as I had

76

two experiences. Relative to our young being led astray, I was struck by a recent issue of *Time* magazine, which referred to America's "dirty mouth pop culture." Two of the articles cautioned how the culture of the '80s and '90s almost by osmosis, encourages lifestyles of indiscriminate sex and violence.

But the second experience again re-enforced that this negative mentoring process is not just a childhood/adolescent problem. At a recent national religious education conference, a middle-age man in attendance stood up and said to a group of us who had given presentations: "I'm torn. I want to be a good Catholic, a good Christian. But I'm also attracted to things and materialism. There's a tug of war going on inside of me." In simple eloquence the man expressed the dilemma of so many of us who are trying to follow the call of the Good Shepherd.

To the degree we fail to positively shepherd each other, to the degree we fail to allow the Good Shepherd to shepherd us, to that degree will we be mentored, shepherded by this generation, the Culture, which, Jesus says, is like a "thief . . . (who) steals, slaughters, and destroys . . ."

"I have come that they might have life," Jesus says, "and have it to the full" (John 10:10).

Patrick J. Brennan

Journal Questions for Individuals and Small Groups

1) a) Read John 10: 1-15
   b) Re-read it, jotting down powerful words and images that strike you
   c) What is the unique message being spoken to you? Jot down notes.
   d) Pray for the courage and grace to live the message, whether comfort or challenge is being spoken to you.

2) What elements of the popular culture, or this generation, do you find most disturbing?

3) How could families and parishes change to better mentor, shepherd young people?

4) How could families and parishes change to better enable adults to mentor adults?

5) How could your small group possibly aid members in:

   — changing society?
   — following the Good Shepherd more closely?

Chapter Seven

"I Will Not Leave You": *Psychological and Spiritual Orphans*

Abandoned Children

WHEN we hear stories on the news of abandoned babies, neonates left on Church steps, in alleys, or even in dumpsters, our hearts are immediately touched. When we hear of a child or children suddenly rendered orphans because of their parents being taken from them through accident, we are moved to pity and compassion. Perhaps more subtle, but nonetheless real, some children rather abruptly lose contact with the non-custodial parent after a divorce. Unfortunately, this is not something the child wants, but something which nonetheless happens. Their pain is less known to us, but indeed such children suffer from *broken hearts* — in fact they often become behavior problems in their remaining families, reconstituted families, or at their schools.

In the fourteenth chapter of John's gospel Jesus uses the metaphor or image of an *orphan*. Specifically, in referring to his return to the Father, he promises that he ". . . will not leave (us) *orphaned* . . ." The word orphan traditionally has been used to describe some of the people and situations described in the first para-

79

Patrick J. Brennan

graph. Let us pause for a moment to reflect on what some of the feelings or internal reactions of an orphan or abandoned child may be.

An orphan or abandoned child frequently has deep-seated feelings of *inadequacy,* or suffers from a *poor self image.* An abandoned child very well may suffer from *anxiety, depression,* and *loneliness.* Often, from the deep recess of the personality, *rage* can spew out. Often if the process of separation from roots has been traumatic, an individual can erect around himself/herself a protective shield, *walling out intimacy, walking in loneliness.*

Anxiety, confusion, depression, rage, poor self image, loneliness — these are just some of the intrapsychic experiences an abandoned child may have acutely or chronically.

A question arises: *why is it that some of us who have never thought of ourselves as orphans have some of the same internal, psychological experiences of anxiety, depression, and loneliness as those who have been actually abandoned?*

Psychological Orphans

A bright, successful thirty-year-old named Tom, sat across from me in the counseling office recently. He has an excellent job, a network of at least superficial friends, an adequate self concept. Yet his presenting symptoms were loneliness, anxiety, depression. He described his success in life as "hollow." Tom is a psychological orphan. Partially he has cut himself off

80

from others through his compulsion for work. Partially the culture or world has done it to him with its norms and expectations. But at least Tom says he would trade all of his success for an intimate relationship. He is a psychological orphan.

A young couple, married just a few years ago, meet regularly with me. She has already outgrown the relationship, and is seeking someone she claims is more her intellectual equivalent. The young man, Ted, is devastated. He still loves Carol. But in the name of self-actualization, she is ready for another relationship. Carol has rendered Ted a psychological orphan.

Tim, a man in mid-life, is divorced. He did not have children with his first wife. Since the divorce, he has had a string of unsuccessful relationships with women, none of them long-lasting. He also has begun to realize that he has no real friends who are male. Tim has growing insight into how he practices "distancing behaviors" with other people, especially women with whom he may become somewhat close. His main way of distancing is through "put down" remarks. Tim can trace this anti-social behavior back to his family of origin. His father was a highly critical put-down artist. He never verbally expressed affection to his family; neither could he hug his children. Tim never remembers being hugged by his father. One *break-through* that we have made in both therapy and his life is to lead him to be able to hug his nephews and nieces. He reports how good it feels to hug and be hugged. He feels he has finally begun to break the "original sin" of his family. But he has a long way to go in recovery. Tim is a psychological orphan.

I have a whole rush of pictures of children that I have seen in counseling over the years. These children were brought to me because of problematic acting-out behaviors either in school or at home. Often when I scratch the surface of symptoms in these childrens' lives, I discover similiar family patterns: five or more hours a day at school; two or more other hours with coaches, teams, or other advisors for some special interest or hobby; some sort of after school supervision or day care; or return to an empty home in late afternoon because either both parents or the custodial parent work. There is, in effect, in the lives of so many of our children too little quality or qualitative time for home or family life. In fact, what kind of modeling is being given to them relative to marriage and family life? So many American children are *psychological orphans!*

And I can see the faces of so many *teens* I have worked with over the years, young people who can *drink* and *drug* with each other and sex with each other. But so many teens have no one with whom they can share their deepest hurts, wounds, questions, or joys. They have *many acquaintances,* but *few friends.* So many adolescents today are psychological orphans.

I'd like to contrast this collage of people and faces with an experience that I recently had. I was giving an evening of renewal for over one hundred liturgical ministers in a parish. One of the discussion/reflection questions that I put to the group was: When was a time that you felt especially close to God? Many striking, inspirational answers were given. But the response of three men especially impressed me. They said their greatest religious experience was their wedding day; for on that day they vowed to God, spouse, and those assembled with them that they would do whatever they had to do to make their marriage and family life work. Their language seemed quite deliberate. They did not want these primary relationships to just last or survive. They wanted them to *work*. Why did their comment and tone strike me?

They sounded like people of a by-gone era. Their primary focus was on the relational. Certainly they had jobs; probably they earned sufficient if not a good deal of money. But things like money or other "vital" concerns of the consumer world were secondary to the importance of their relationships.

Why are there so many psychological orphans in our culture? I think as a society we have lost sufficient concern for our relational worlds. This loss of concern has mass-produced people who can "be with," can be in a crowd, but nonetheless feel alone in life. This is at the *core* of being a psychological orphan. There very well may be people in one's life, but a person feels alone, estranged, alienated, or has diminished capacity for intimacy or relationships, or has been robbed somehow, of the opportunity.

A psychiatrist friend of mine reflected on this recently. He attributed the estrangement and loneliness

Patrick J. Brennan

that I am speaking of to the break down of the family. He spoke of family broadly, however. Has the nuclear family been severely damaged? Of course, he would say. But family as a network of close concerned relationships has collapsed quite extensively. He is referring rather to the family of *neighborhood, extended family, parish or Church,* and *on and on.* A recent U.S. bishop's statement, *A Family Perspective in Church and Society* has suggested much the same thing that the psychiatrist said. The bishops' statement says that even in parish programs and ministries, the Church is now mirroring the world in its pre-occupation with the individual. We minister to individuals, rather than to individuals and "their social context," or network of primary relationships. The bishops' statement calls for a return to a new relational, social, familial lens to be used in planning and evaluating parish ministries. In his book *The Social Imperative,* Gregory Baum in 1979, prophetically called for a retrieval of the essentially social character of the gospel message.

"All the lonely people" the Beatles sang years ago, "where do they come from?"

An Attempt at An Answer: Eros vs. Agape

Antiquity, pre-Christian and Christian, distinguished between two kinds of love: *eros* and *agape. Eros* is a self-focused love. A person values or stays with a relationship for what the other person can do for him or her. There is always "pay off" in an eros-type relationship. *Agape* refers to a much more selfless, spiritual

84

kind of love. In agape, people in a relationship are trying to help each other become the best, most wholistic self one can be. In the language of Christianity, agape is self-sacrificial love, oriented toward helping another discover his or her true vocation or calling, the *self* God intended the person to be from the moment of conception in the womb.

Why do we have all these psychological orphans? Because the world is shot through with *eros,* and not enough *agape.* Agape is the love "of the cross"; it is Paul's notion of Kenosis or self emptying for others, which Jesus did perfectly. In this psychological age, people shy away from agape, because we have been taught by one self-help book after another to not allow ourselves to be anyone's door mat.

Again, the movement toward self-actualization (which is a good in itself), has made talk of self sacrificial love sound almost neurotic. The fact is *agape* can only be engaged in by strong people, non-neurotic types who are assured enough in and of themselves that they want to invest in the life of another.

One of my favorite T.V. shows has been *The Wonder Years.* If the reader is unfamiliar with it, the show tells the story of the adolescent awakening of a young boy, Kevin Arnold, in the late sixties, early seventies. The story is narrated by an adult actor who is understood to be Kevin as a grown man looking back at this adolescent transition in his life. Kevin is desperately in love with Winnie Cooper, a lovely young girl who lives on his block. The finale of a recent episode involved the announcement that Winnie's family was selling the house and moving. Winnie's new house will only be four miles away, but Kevin is nonetheless devastated. He says that four miles for a thirteen year old is like a trip from New York to Paris. The final scene of the show has Kevin on his bike, ready for his first four mile, New York to Paris trip to Winnie's house. In hindsight, the adult Kevin says "Before Winnie Cooper, I thought the whole world was outside my door. But I discovered that, because of Winnie, my world had to expand and get larger."

People with an agape love for each other constantly enlarge their world to include the other despite life's changes, stages, and developments. Agape love is constantly expanding, inclusive, other centered love. Without it, giving and getting it, humans are rendered psychological orphans.

Spiritual Orphans

In their book *Megatrends 2000,* John Naisbitt and Patricia Aburdene predict that the '90s and the turn of the century will experience a new spiritual awakening, a new quest for spirituality and meaning. If they are accurate, Jesus's words in the fourteenth chapter of John have special importance and comfort for me. "I will never leave you orphaned, I will remain with and in you." Jesus explains; as He is in the Father and the Father is in Him, so we can remain in him and he in us. And the medium through which this is experienced is the Holy Spirit. The Holy Spirit is the experience of the Father and the Son always with us and within us — not with eros but rather agape love.

If physical or psychological abandonment can produce anxiety, meaningless, depression, loneliness and other problematic emotional states in people, these conditions are multiplied and maximized in people who have never met the Lord's love personally. In reality, we are an age of functional idolators, atheists, and agnostics. We, in effect, live in a post-Christian, post-atheistic age, says James Fitzpatrick in an analysis of Austrialian and Western society. To not live under the gentle sway of the Spirit, to be in communion with God's unconditional love, with grace, is to be a situation of chronic existential angst.

The *challenge* inherent in this chapter's reflection is to stop abandoning, psychologically orphan-ing each other, to love each other with "agape love." The *comfort* of this chapter is a reminder that the Spirit of God will never orphan us. We need only recognize the power of the Spirit in our daily lives, and upon recognizing it, to cooperate with and surrender to it.

I was told recently that some of these thoughts were too critical of people entering into, staying with, or terminating relationships. The question put to me was "Do you really think people consciously enter into relationships with the intent to hurt each other?" "No," I responded, "but I want to underscore your own word *consciously*." I wish more people would become more *conscious* of the anti-relationship, anti-commitment forces that are undermining American society.

Patrick J. Brennan

Journal Questions for Individuals and Small Groups

1) Most of us have 20-25 relationships that are rooted in kinship, geographical proximity, school, work or other hobbies and interests, that constitute our primary relationships. Think out or write down a list of the primary people in your life. Evaluate the quality of each of the relationships.

2) What could you change about *you* to become more effective in relating?

3) This chapter is a reflection on the quality of American relationships. What steps need to be taken by couples to improve the quality of American marriages?

4) What steps need to be taken by parents to improve the quality of American family life?

5) How does the parish need to change to better minister to singles?

Chapter Eight

A Church In Passage
Chaos: The Original Model of Church

"... A sound like to blowing of a violent wind came from heaven and filled the whole house where they were ... What seemed to be tongues of fire ... came to rest on each of them. All of them were filled with the Holy Spirit ... Peter stood up ... and addressed the crowd: "Fellow Jews and all of you who live in Jerusalem ... listen carefully to what I say ... Jesus of Nazareth was a man accredited to you by miracles, wonders, and signs, which God did among you through Him ... (He) was handed over to you by God's set purpose ... you, with the help of wicked men, put him to death by nailing him to the cross. But God raised him from the dead, freeing him from the agony of death, because it was impossible for death to keep its hold on him. When the people heard this, they were cut to the heart and said to Peter ... "What shall we do?" Peter replied, 'Repent and be baptized ... in the name of Jesus Christ for the forgiveness of your sins. And you will receive the gift of the Holy Spirit.' Those who accepted his message were baptized, and about three thousand were added to their number that day ... They devoted themselves to the apostles teaching and to fellowship, to the breaking of the bread and to

Patrick J. Brennan

prayer . . . All the believers . . . held everything in common . . . they gave to anyone as he/she had need. Every day they continued to meet together in the temple courts. They broke bread in their houses, and ate together with glad and sincere hearts, praising God . . . And the Lord added to their number daily those who were being saved . . . (Acts 2:2-47).

A PRIEST friend of mine frequently calls with the recurring analysis of the state of the Church: "Brennan, the wheels are coming off the cart." I respond in kind: "We'll probably be God's two last priests; one of us will have to turn off the lights." Half cynical, half frightened, my friend and I are responding to the news so characteristic of the Church these days: priests continue to leave active church ministry; the supply of priests, sisters, and other full-time religious who used to staff parishes continues to diminish; in some dioceses only about a quarter of the potential congregation worships; the numbers problem has created a stewardship problem — no people, no money, limited ministries. The Church as we once knew it is in chaos. The recent rash of closings and mergings of parishes, schools, and seminaries in both Detroit and Chicago are indicators of the chaos that we are in.

But *chaos* ought not to carry with it the *negative* connotations that it usually does. The Yahwist author of the book of *Genesis* describes earth at the beginning of time as a "formless wasteland, with darkness covering the abyss, while mighty winds swept over the waters. . . ." That description plus the account that follows of God bringing forth creation make an important theological statement: God draws *creation* out of *chaos.* Chaos can often be a movement of the Spirit leading to creation. The Pentecost experience of Acts 2, which we began with, the movement of the Holy Spirit is first experienced as a chaotic surge that then gave rise to a new Creation — the Church of Jesus Christ.

In the apparent chaos of today's Church scene, God's Spirit is again at work among his people, transforming chaos into a new creation. In fact, we are experiencing, are part of, a great mystery, a mystery bigger than the closing and merging of some institutions, as heart wrenching as that may be for many people. I believe that we are experiencing what Vincent Donovan describes in his book, *The Church in the Midst of Creation,* the death of the "Industrial Revolution" parish. The Industrial Revolution parish can be housed in either old buildings or new ones, but such a parish reflects the spirit of the Industrial Revolution. The Industrial Revolution produced *assembly line operations* in the world of business, resulting in things like greater productivity, organization, and quality and quantity control. The words Donovan uses to describe the factory are "centralization, synchronization, organization, specialization, and maximization."

Some of these attributes of the Industrial Revolution

found their way into the Catholic parish of the twentieth century. These attributes and values expressed themselves in parish programs, in the traditional parish school, CCD program, parish organizations; and since the '60s, '70s, and '80s, they have expressed themselves in parish *volunteer* ministries. Donovan feels, and I agree, that we are experiencing the death of the Industrial Revolution parish which ran and runs people through programs, catechetical training, and organizations. The good news is that the death of that kind of parish, which was good for its day, is giving birth to a new style of parish, one closer in style to the Christian community, born out of the chaos of the movement of the Holy Spirit on Pentecost, than it is to the Industrial Revolution parish.

Attention

The bishops of Alta/Baja California recently wrote a pastoral on the issue of the crisis of evangelicals, cults, and proselytizers attracting huge numbers of Catholics, who have grown disenchanted with their own Church. With clear vision, the bishops accurately described the situation in many Catholic — and also mainline Protestant — parishes or congregations. They explained that current pastoral approaches have "inadequate structures" for effective evangelization. These inadequate structures are the residue of the dying Industrial Revolution Church. These inadequate structures, the bishops add, fail to provide the *personal attention* to people that is needed for effective evangelization and ministry. In other words, an Industrial Revolution parish may have been, may be efficient in management of numbers of people, but it is deficient in offering personal attention. Psychologist Abraham Maslow said years ago that people gravitate to situations or organizations that gratify their self-actualization, self-esteem and belonging needs. The Church of guilt and obligation has its caboose in the mid-forties demographic group. Younger believers, Catholic and Protestant, will go where they are fed, will go where they feel they belong. This is the insight of the Alta/Baja bishops and a growing conviction of mine.

To remedy the impersonal nature of the Industrial Revolution parish, the bishops make specific recommendations for personalizing, warming up the maintenance-locked parish. Their recommendations speak of the mysterious new creation of parish, which is congruent with the Church of Pentecost. The bishops suggest: 1) divide the typical parish up into regions or districts with deacons, deaconal couples, or lay people serving as overseers; 2) further sub-divide these districts into small Christian communities, wherein adults and families meet to share and pray; 3) begin pro-active attempts at non-proselytizing, but pastoral home visits.

The are many reasons for people absenting themselves from the Table of the Lord. But I believe the bishops are accurate in highlighting the personal attention issue. The demise of the Industrial Revolution parish is indeed painful for many, but it is nonetheless a painful prologue to the coming of a new creation. We need to co-operate with the Holy Spirit in this potential New Pentecost.

Hispanic Wisdom

The authors of the *National Pastoral Plan for Hispanic Ministry,* likewise have insights into and glimpse what the coming, new Pentecostal church will look like. Planning for future ministry to Hispanics and recent immigrants to this country, they wrote:

1) ministries in a parish are often compartmentalized and fragmented; there must be a new co-ordination and convergence of ministries towards evangelization;

2) the often anonymous large Catholic congregation must be transformed from a *place* to a *home;* this can best be done through the proliferation of small groups of the Church in homes;

3) in a spirit of missionary zeal, we must move from *pews* to a better use of *shoes* in bringing Christ and the Church into our neighborhood and the world;

4) (perhaps their most insightful comment) none of the above will happen, in fact, evangelization remains mere *good will,* if serious steps are not taken toward planning and equipping more and more people with skills for evangelization and pastoral ministry.

PASCHAL JOURNEY

A Synthesis

The March 23, 1990 edition of the *Explorer*, the Joliet, Illinois diocesan newspaper contained recommendations from its 1989 synod. The first priority of the diocese, flowing from the synod's deliberations, is to better evangelize.To that end, the synod strongly recommended the following:

1) Better outreach processes, especially to those in spiritual and personal need;

2) Processes of re-entry for those who want to return to the Catholic Church;

3) Better welcoming processes for new parishioners;

4) Better youth and young adult evangelization, with preparation for the Sacrament of Confirmation modeled on the dynamics and ministries of the Rite of Christian Initiation of Adults;

5) Better evangelization of families via religious education. This implies adaptation of traditional parochical school models and what is typically referred to as CCD. The school and/or religious education program should, in effect, try to minister to/evangelize the social context of the child, rather than just the child;

6) An endorsement of the dynamics of the Rite of Christian Initiation of Adults as the core dynamics of spiritual renewal to be brought in every parish effort and ministry. These steps or dy-

namics include an opportunity for forming relationships with fellow believers' (evangelization or re-evangelization, that is being invited to accept Jesus as Lord and the faith community as the body of Christ) time for ongoing faith formation and information; opportunities for spiritual purification and direction; an ongoing invitation to commitment and conversion; and, *no graduation,* that is, a conviction that the process ends by beginning again, over and over again;

7) Better preaching and more life-enriching liturgical celebration;

8) The proliferation and support of small faith sharing groups;

9) Better inculturation efforts, that is, ministry that is respectful of African-American, Hispanic, and Asian immigrants; this was certainly how our ancestors found faith rootedness in this country;

10) Ongoing prayer for and consciousness of the larger missionary activity of the Church around the world.

We are a church in chaos, but the three documents that I cited above are glimmers of hope in the midst of chaos for me.

What receives so much media attraction in our church as "death" can really be resurrection and new life! The Spirit, I believe is drawing a "new creation of church" out of the chaos of recent years. The Spirit is moving our Church, our parishes, back to the dynamics of the Church born on Pentecost. We need to co-operate with the Holy Spirit, in a posture of discernment, courage and reasonable risk taking and action.

The opposite of such a posture is to try to repair the non-repairable. We saw some of the later approaches recently in some of the leaders of the Soviet Union. Rather than face the bankrupt nature of the Soviet structures, some tried to repair them. They are irreparable. The fall of the Berlin Wall; the nationalism of Lithuania and the Baltic states; the rise of Russian nationalism/and President Yeltsin in Russia, ended the Soviet Union. Democratic surges in these nations, Romania, Poland, and elsewhere do not speak to me so much about people power as much as they do about the movement of the Holy Spirit. Totalitarian regimes can keep people shackled for a while, but eventually the Spirit of God, flowing through people, throws the status quo into chaos.

The Church, specifically the institutional model of church, cannot expect to be immune from the Spirit's chaos — new creation movement. We also can waste time trying to repair the irreparable. I believe we need to go with the Spirit's flow. That Spirit seems to be re-creating a Pentecostal church, a church in which:

- as Peter did, there is bold and clear evangelization;
- sacraments are again celebrations of conversion;
- experiences in large church (parish Eucharistic

assembly) are also joined to multiple opportunities for church in the home and family;

- the entire people of God feel co-responsible to co-labor in ministry and works of justice.

If we co-operate with the Spirit, rather than holding on to the status quo in an addictive way, I am convinced, day by day, the Lord will add to our number.

Personal Pentecost: From Chaos to Creation

The chaos — new creation process is going on on a large scale, ecclesially, globally; but it also goes on quite personally in each of our lives. The experience is variously described as conversion, transformation, or as I did above, personal Pentecost. As I have written in previous books, I believe God is at work in each of our lives manifesting, showing himself to us. This is ongoing *revelation*. I also believe that in the matrix of human experience and relationships, God is calling us, deep within our hearts and souls. This is ongoing *vocation*. We can anesthesize ourselves to such revelation and vocation phenomena. In fact, Allen Bloom, in *The Closing of the American Mind,* says that America has become increasingly non-reflective, a phenomenon that indeed impedes *discerning revelation and vocation.*

From Babel to Pentecost

As in the case of the Church in general, becoming a new creation often involves a Tower of Babel, a period of chaos. Though conversion, transformation, a new Pentecost can occur in life's joy moments and experiences, much research concurs that usually there has to be a kind of break-down in one's life for a person to begin to surrender to the sway and force of the Holy Spirit. The threshold for conversion, often an experience of chaos, can have to do with one's health, emotions, relationships. career, addictions, sin, indeed almost any human experience can be the context in which a new creation can begin to emerge. It is important to always keep in mind that in these processes which can be days, months, or years, in length, we do not control the process. Just as the first Pentecost was an experience of the first believers being grasped by someone more than themselves, so also are personal Pentecost experiences. As truth emerges relative to God's revelation, one's calling or vocation, as the nature of the gifts a person shares in by the power of the Holy Spirit emerges, the challenge or quest a person is confronted with is to be obedient to the truth, God's truth, as it seems to be emerging in a person's life. This obedience is at first experienced as pain. It involves some self-emptying. But remaining faithful to the process of being led by the Spirit eventually leads one to a new Pentecost, to new creation.

Change

In the fourteenth chapter of John's gospel, Jesus says to his apostles that he must leave so that the Spirit can come. He goes on to say that he knows that they do

Patrick J. Brennan

not understand now. But he insists, it is best that he leave, so that the Spirit can come. In effect, he is saying "You do not understand this change now, because you are in the midst of it. But do not resist the change, for ultimately good will come from it."

It was the physicist Isaac Newton who said: "Moving bodies seek to continue moving; bodies at rest seek to remain at rest." Through physics, Newton was communicating a profound insight into the nature of most organisms and creatures: *we do not like change.* Whatever course that we are on — even if it is not too healthy or there is a greater good — we like to stay on that course. We are creatures of comfort and habit.

So also were the post resurrection, pre-Pentecost followers of Jesus. More than creatures of comfort and habit, they were crippled with fear, meaninglessness, and a loss of direction. When they allowed themselves to be grasped by a power greater than themselves, however, they were transformed into people of courage, action, and vision. Change becomes less fear-filled, less resisted by us if we believe that in least some of life's changes there is present and active for us divine Spirit, both revealing and calling.

Dusting off the Gifts of
The Holy Spirit

Rather than running from change, personal Pentecost, conversion, we ought to seek it out in our lives. Daily we ought to invite the Spirit in to lead, guide, direct, and heal us. Those gifts or contributions that are traditionally ascribed to God's spirit, we ought to pray for daily: wisdom, understanding, counsel, fortitude, knowledge, piety, and awe or reverence for God. Truly they are more life giving dominant images to influence our lives, than some of the dominant images of the culture or the society around us which often rob us of life rather than integrate us.

The New Creation of Church and world can happen through you and me, under the guidance of the Holy Spirit, beginning with our own personal Pentecost, conversion, transformation, change. In John 3, Jesus tells Nicodemus that we need to be baptized in water and the Spirit to see God's reign. Unfortunately, many of us who have been baptized in water have yet to be baptized in the Holy Spirit. If baptism or confirmation was not personal Pentecost for any of us, we would do well to pray for the outpouring of that Spirit each day.

Journal Questions for Individuals and Small Groups

1) A gift of the Holy Spirit is an ability given to me not just from self aggrandizement, but for the common good and to give glory to God. Write down how you have been gifted. Be specific.

2) Are you in any ways burned out because you are involved in things for which you are not gifted, thus burning out?

3) Are you rusting out, not using gifts that the Spirit has given you?

Patrick J. Brennan

4) What are feelings in the group about the Alta/ Baja, Hispanic, and Joliet Synod comments about the status of Church?

5) Where do you see the Spirit working in the world and Church today effecting a new Pentecost?

6) How does the closing discussion about the need for all of us to be born again and baptized in the Holy Spirit make you feel?

Chapter Nine

More Chaos Beyond the Anonymous Crowd

IN THEIR book *Children at Risk — The Battle for the Health and Minds of Our Kids,* Dr. James Dobson and Gary Bauer speak of mourning not only the millions of babies taken from their place of safety, by abortion these past years, but also of mourning all of today's children permitted to live. The children permitted to live will not have an easy journey, they say. The core of the twisted philosophy that permitted and permits abortion now prevails in the Western World. Society, they suggest, is incredibly dangerous to the inner worlds of our children; toxic pressures now engulf most children. In elementary school, our children learn, by cultural osmosis, that virginity is a "curse" and sex an "adolescent toy." Even if a child or teen wanted to remain chaste today, he or she is made to feel like a "prude" or "freak." In effect, the media simply evangelizes, "everybody is 'doing it' today."

Recently, in a radio interview, Chicago media critic, Gary Deeb, deplored the current state of children's television. Cartoons and non-animated shows frequently display gratuitous violence as a way to solve problems. Besides such obvious messages, some shows are created simply to sell products. The goal of either kind of program is to get to the commercials to convince the young *what* they absolutely must have to be happy. Commercials oriented to the older, lucrative late teen, '20s or '30s group, connect feminine beauty, masculinity and being in good shape with drinking "lite-beer" and wine coolers. Deeb said the message is clear: drinking is fun and sexy, done on beaches, boats, and in parks with accompanying pet dogs and frizbees. The sadder truth, however, said Deeb, is that the advertisers are appealing most to teens, trying to prepare them to drink, to convince them of the connection between a good image and alcohol consumption.

Dobson and Bauer say that, indeed, we are in the midst of the second American Civil War, with two major value systems clashing: that of materialistic consumerism, and the Gospel, or Kingdom living. The former has become a hostile culture that makes it difficult for parents, teachers, and religious educators to do their jobs. Parents, especially, they say, need to become better sensitized to what their children see, read, hear, and do.

Dr. Jane Healy in *Endangered Minds — Why Our Children Don't Think,* postulates that children's brains have been seriously altered, if not damaged, by the barrage of TV, video, and computer games. Children's minds have become passive with diminished attention; they cannot manage their own thinking. Also children have poor social skills, since they interact less and less with adults and other children, and more and more with automated things.

The critical analyses continue to flow from thinkers and clinicians. Dr. Toni Saunders, who runs the Capable Kid counselling center, based in Evanston, Illinois, postulates that if present trends continue, the profile for a class of 40 graduating teens in the year 2000 might look something like this:

- 2 of the class will give birth before graduation;
- 8 will drop out of school;
- 11 will be unemployed after graduation;
- 15 will end up living in poverty;
- by graduation, 36 will have used alcohol, 17 marijuana, and 8 will have used cocaine;
- 6 will have run away;
- at least one will have died by his or her own hand, that is, through suicide;

Dr. Robert Coles, in *The Spiritual Life of Children,* speaks of our age as a neo-Victorian age in which we are repressing not so much sexuality as we are spirituality. He sees children as inherently spiritual, but the increasingly anemic state of adult faith in America is burying natural childhood spirituality.

The October 8, 1990 issue of *Time* magazine conveyed even more realistic figures, statistics about America *now:* every eight seconds a child drops out of school; every 26 seconds a child runs away from home; every 47 seconds, a child is abused or neglected; every 67 seconds a teenager has a baby; every seven minutes a child is arrested for a drug offense; every

Patrick J. Brennan

36 minutes a child is killed or injured by a gun; every day, 135,000 children bring guns to school. These statistics, say the authors, reflect not just urban poor, but also young people from the most comfortable surroundings. The article suggests that such hurting children may very well turn, in retaliation, on the world that caused so much pain. The November 5, 1990 issue of *People* adds that seven out of ten American adolescents are sexually active, despite the threat of AIDS.

The Young as a Barometer

The foregoing is not intended just as a reflection on the state of American youth. It is intended, rather, to see children and teens as a barometer, or reflection, of what is going on in American living and culture. Especially those of us interested in spirituality, or ministry, must realize that we do not do either ministry or spirituality in a vacuum. We serve others and seek God in a context called *culture.* I am suggesting that increasly American culture is post-Christian. The work of evangelization, then, is never a matter of "me and Jesus" or "my clique and Jesus." The real challenge to the Church for the future is to evangelize this post-Christian culture.

The Power of Image

I think we begin to evangelize or transform culture by beginning to pay more and more attention to the power of dominant directive images. Indeed, we live life, propelled a great deal by our imaginations. In this sense, I am speaking of imagination as the deposit of those images, dreams, and heart wishes that influence how we live. For a good number of years, for example, the dominant images of fear, worry, and the need to control dominated my imagination, and, therefore, how I lived my life. Gradually, over the course of the years, with a lot of personal effort and also help from others, those dominant images became or at least skewed more toward trust, hope and surrender.

As we possess intra-psychic dominant images, so also we are barraged by cultural images. John Kavanaugh, S.J., lists some of them in *Following Christ in a Consumer Society*. They are:

- sexuality is mechanical;
- your body is a machine;
- fear/threat;
- don't be committed;
- retain yourself;
- learn techniques;
- stay on the externals of life;
- all people are replaceable;
- be cool;
- be hard;
- accumulate;
- be invulnerable;
- hedonism; gratify every pleasure;
- have;
- be content with what is;

107

- be skeptical;
- doubt;
- independence;
- isolation;
- addiction;
- it all ends in death anyway.

Pretty grim, are they not? Yet young people and adults in a sense, breathe in those dominant images like air pollution daily. It is time that we developed a more wholistic sense of what faith is.

- Faith is intellectual: there is a certain body of tradition we ought to know, if we are to be literate about our faith.
- Faith is relational, involving a personal relationship with God, and a faith community.
- Faith is performative. Because we believe, we ought to live in a certain way.
- Faith, also, is imaginitive. It involves living those directive, dominant images that Jesus lived and preached about, under the umbrella of "The Kingdom", or "The Reign of God."

Part of getting to Jesus's dominant images is to begin to surface, name, critique, and offer alternatives to the counter-gospel images of the culture.

The Call to Holiness

The post-Christian culture I have been referring to is crying out for a renewed call to holiness. Growing up, many of us who are middle-aged or older wanted to be holy. Jesuit writer, William O'Malley recently wrote that young people today would gladly accept epithets like "gay," "slut," or "bi-sexual" over holy. Maybe that is because the Church has too much made "other worldly" the notion of holiness. Holiness is rather about deep, loving immersion into *this world*. If we look at the holiness of Jesus in the Scriptures we see someone who: 1) was regular in the practice of prayer and solitude; 2) was connected to a faith tradition and community; 3) moved from prayer and community to the world, especially to the poor, the broken, the underside of society to heal and transform. Jesus was much more of an activist than we traditionally thought him to be. In imitation of Christ, we need a balance in our lives of what Thomas Merton called "the journey inward" and "the journey outward."

Beyond the Anonymous Crowd

If we as a Church are to adequately respond to and evangelize society and culture, then we need to change our ecclesiology, or our image of Church, that in turn dictates how we do Church. The felt experience of Church for too many is that of an anonymous crowd, some of whom gather weekly to watch the "Christian super-stars, both ordained and non-ordained" *do* their thing. The parish campus can be quickly left after an hour and in reality, forgotten, until the next gathering of what we so glibly refer to as "community." As

Patrick J. Brennan

a church, "the crowd" motif is killing us. If, as *Newsweek* of December 17, 1990 says, there seems to be a renewed seeking of churches on the part of the baby-boomers, "crowd" churches are not magnetic forces. Churches wherein community is real are attractive forces. Quoting a recent Lilly Endowment study conducted by Wade Clark Roof and David Roozen, the article says denominationalism is not the pull that it once was. Those forty and younger are attracted rather by the quality of spirituality and ministry offered by a Church. Thus, many do not so much leave the Church as they do cross denominations to become part of a parish or congregation where they are fed. The Catholic *crowd* needs to become a Church of *disciples, apostles and prophets, sympathizers, and stewards.* Briefly, let us examine each of those realities.

- *A Church of disciples:* In his critique of American educational systems, *Giants and Dwarfs*, Allan Bloom maintains that no one really learns until they become someone's disciple. A disciple subordinates his own ego to share in the greater wisdom of a master. In our case, the master is Jesus. Christian discipleship is a journey, from which there is no graduation. It is life-long. Disciples are often imperfect and slow to learn, but the appropriation of content is not as important for disciples as is picking up the values, images, and wisdom of the master. In a Church of discipleship, we all,

110

ideally, would be in a mentoring relationship. The mentor would be Jesus.

- *A church of apostles and prophets:* Apostleship is a step beyond discipleship. It involves, as the first apostles did, taking Christ to the marketplace, to the world. We run *from* the world *to* Church. Jesus would have us reverse the process, and leave our churches to renew the world. Such a heroic effort involves young people, in the context of their peers at school, having an obvious relationship with Christ and the Church, and being critical about the media and the culture. Apostleship would involve adults trying to bring the values of the Kingdom and the person of Christ to work, the marketplace and the neighborhood. Prophecy would involve a critical, reflective spirit — knowing what to say yes and no to in our culture.

- *A church of stewards:* All of God's people are charismatic, gifted. Ministry is using one's giftedness to usher in the Kingdom. It is not done by a few ordained, credentialed, trained elite. Neither does the use of one's gifts need to wait for an appropriate age (eg.18); nor should gifts be wasted in meaningless tasks like some childrens' Confirmation service projects. As early as possible, every member of God's family ought to be encouraged to discern one's giftedness and to use those gifts

111

wisely, as good stewards, to serve others and give glory to God.

- *A church of sympathizers:* The sympathizers were those like Martha, Mary, Lazarus, and Zachaeus who welcomed Jesus into their homes. As more and more talk goes toward small groups, and base communities, it would be good if more practical talk were oriented toward how people can live the dynamics of Church first on the level of primary relationships. Whether those relationships be by blood or by choice, it is in the family where relationships are first modeled, values are picked up almost by osmosis, meals are shared, and time is spent. Large church, that is the Eucharistic assembly, will never make sense until communion, or Church is first experienced on the level of home or family.

Becoming, more deliberately, a Church, a parish of disciples, apostles, prophets, stewards, and sympathizers would dramatically alter the face and felt experience of Church.

Pentecost Dynamics

As I mentioned in the previous chapter, on the day of its birth, the Church was characterized by movement of the Holy Spirit, bold evangelization, conversion of life joined to sacraments, people meeting in large groups, as well as meeting also in small groups, in homes; and all, not a few ministering. In this *Acts*

PASCHAL JOURNEY

2, Pentecostal model of Church "daily the Lord added to their number." I believe the Holy Spirit is moving in us, edging us "back to the future." Indeed it seems often like the church is dying, especially the large, mainline churches. In fact, it is part of the churches being on the paschal journey, dying but also growing toward new life.

Journal Questions for Individuals and Small Groups

1) To what degree, in what ways do I/we operate out of cultural dominant images rather than those of the Reign of God?

2) Rate yourself in terms of living out these identities: Disciple? Apostle? Prophet? Steward? Sympathizer?

3) In what specific ways does being in a small group improve our over-all experience of Church?

4) Do the studies mentioned at the beginning of the chapter (eg. Donovan) congruently describe dominant culture; or do they over-state the problem?

Chapter Ten

Adult Children of Alcoholics

The Twelve Steps

1. We admitted we were powerless over alcohol — that our lives had become unmanageable.

2. Came to believe that a Power greater than ourselves could restore us to sanity.

3. Made a decision to turn our will and our lives over to the care of God as we understood Him.

4. Made a searching and fearless moral inventory of ourselves.

5. Admitted to God, to ourselves and to another human being the exact nature of our wrongs.

6. Were entirely ready to have God remove all these defects of character.

7. Humbly asked Him to remove our shortcomings.

8. Made a list of all persons we had harmed, and became willing to make amends to them all.

9. Made direct amends to such people wherever possible, except when to do so would injure them or others.

10. Continued to take personal inventory and when we were wrong, promptly admitted it.

11. *Sought through prayer and meditation to improve our conscious contact with God, as we understood Him, praying only for knowledge of His will for us and the power to carry that out.*

12. *Having had a spiritual awakening as a result of these steps, we tried to carry this message to others and to practice these principles in all our affairs.*

Original Sin Re-Visited

Original sin is a theological formulation that has been bouncing around Judaeo — Christian thinking (though not always so labeled) for thousands of years. The most traditional Christain explanation is that through the sin of Adam and Eve a given quantum of evil is passed on in birth — an evil that can only be washed away or remedied by the waters of Baptism. Most of us who are over 40 remember the likes of black and white milk bottles as metaphors used to explain the once and for all removal of original sin by the pouring of baptismal water.

As I have aged, become a psychotherapist, and allowed psychological skills and theological reflection to blend with each other, I have begun to reinterpret original sin in a different way. While I would not like to offer the following for critique by moral theologians, I do think there is a modicum of truth in it. At least part of the mystery of original sin, or the ontic, "already out there" evil, is the fact that we pass on *crippling, dysfunctional attitudes and ways of life from*

115

one generation to another in our family systems. There is growing research into and evidence of anxiety-prone and/or depression prone parents handing such tendencies on to their children. Alcoholism is increasingly being studied as a phenomenon that potentially can be passed on genetically. Approximately 50% of adolescents who commit suicide, do so under the influence of drugs and alcohol; and 80% of adolescent suicides are children of alcoholics.

Evil is not so much a metaphysical thing, spiritually transmitted via intercourse and childbirth. Evil is, also, at least in part, the hurtful, dysfunctional style of *relating* to others that often is passed on from one generation to another in families. In this chapter, we will focus specifically on how the disease of alcoholism influences an entire family system. Our focus will not be so much on how alcoholism is possibly genetically transmitted as much as on how the disease of alcoholism in one member definitely influences the attitudes, behavioral patterns and relational style of all family members.

Co-Alcoholism

A young adult, a single man, came to see me recently. His mother is an alcoholic. He has coped with, adapted himself, molded himself, over and over again, to fit his mother's alcohol-determined mood swings and erratic behavior. What troubles him now is that he feels a rage, an uncontrollable rage, a seething resentment within growing toward his mother. He is afraid of these feelings, afraid that he might act on them eventually.

This young man was surprised when I placed a label on his emotional situation recently. I called him a co-alcoholic. He was at first confused and mystified by the term. I tried to explain the dynamics of co-dependence.

The family members of an alcoholic, or anyone in a primary relationship with an alcoholic, become addicted in his or her own way. They become addicted to the toxic relational system mandated and created by the alcoholic. Claudia Black, author of *It Will Never Happen to Me* and other publications, and a pioneer in the Adult Children of Alcoholics Movement, describes the growing children of alcoholics as taking on several distinct personality types. Some deny reality and are able to hide, repress the family secret of alcoholism from themselves and others. Others take on an overly responsible caretaking role, feeling they can somehow, correct or right the wrongs of the addictive family system. Perhaps the most healthy have the most obvious problems. They are the ones who rebel — acting out at home and/or at school, but nonetheless, saying through their acting out that they resent and refuse to comply with the addictive family system.

Likewise, the spouse of an alcoholic also often takes on a role — most frequently that of *enabler.* In the name of love, he or she may cover for the alcoholic, make excuses for his or her behavior, organize the

family system so that the alcoholic's drinking goes un-
challenged. These child and spousal patterns are what
we mean by co-dependency. Everyone in such a family
system finds his or her identity from the drinker and
his or her problem. Sharon Wegscheider-Cruse defines
co-dependence as an addiction to another person or
persons and their problems or to a relationship and
its problems (quoted in *When Society Becomes An Addict,* Anne Wilson Schaef, p. 29).

In speaking with a mid-life woman recently, I described some of the characteristics of adult children
of alcoholics. She and her husband had come for marriage counseling, unaware of how the co-alcoholism
or co-dependency with her father, who was an alcoholic, years ago, was influencing her individual and
relational life in the present. Before any marriage
therapy could transpire, there would have to be a lot
of individual therapy to get her in touch with her
ACOA patterns. I told the woman that adult children
of alcoholics:

- are often isolated and afraid of people and authority figures;
- are approval seekers, losing identity in the
  process;
- are frightened by feelings of anger and any
  criticism leveled toward them;
- marry alcoholics, become alcoholics, or merge
  with and co-operate with someone else with a
  compulsive personality disorder;

- become super responsible or super-irresponsible;
- develop guilt feelings over self expression;
- are addicted or accustomed to excitement and upset; don't know what normalcy feels like;
- confuse love and pity and tend to call the pity they have toward the addicted "love";
- learn to "stuff" feelings, beginning in a traumatic childhood, and therefore fail to learn the ability to express feelings throughout most of one's lifetime, unless there is some intervention;
- judge the self harshly, and have very low feelings of self-esteem;
- are often dependent (in an unhealthy sense) personalities, with almost child-like, indeed infantile fears of abandonment; this chronic fear of abandonment stems from significant adults, trapped in the alcoholic system, never really being there for the growing child;
- have difficulty having fun;
- are often procrastinators in accomplishing a project;
- take the self too seriously;
- are extremely loyal (addicted?) even when such loyalty is obviously undeserved;
- over-react to change;
- are often impulsive, acting without considering options; therefore, much time is spent in guilt, self-

loathing, and cleaning up messes that need not have been there to begin with;

- look for immediate rather than deferred gratification;
- over-react out of fear.

As I mentioned some of the characteristics of ACOA's, the mid-life woman's jaw dropped. She could identify with 95% of what I shared with her. Gradually she saw, became convinced that she needed to begin to change herself, attend ACOA meetings, work her own spiritual program, and maybe a bit later, get to the marriage problems.

This woman was interesting in her secondary reaction. Her face grew red; her hands trembled, and she said "I'm angry. I'm angry that I'm co-alcoholic, or co-dependent, or whatever you call it!" There is not a lot to say to ameliorate or soften that feeling. If addiction is a disease, a few of us chose any disease. We have to, rather, work through the stages of grief in eventually coming to some sort of acceptance of the situation, and a hopeful new beginning.

Further Characteristics

Dr. Jean Woititz in *Adult Children of Alcoholics* isolates intra and inter — personal characteristics of the alcoholic:

- excessive dependency,
- inability to express emotion,

- low frustration tolerance,
- emotional immaturity,
- a high level of anxiety in interpersonal relationships,
- low self-esteem,
- grandiosity,
- perfectionism,
- feelings of isolation,
- ambivalence toward authority,
- guilt,

She goes on to say that, whether an adult child becomes a problem drinker or not, he or she goes on to mirror some of these *same* intra/inter-personal patterns. Typically, like the alcoholic, the ACOA is too *self-focused,* with tremendous barriers up against intimacy.

Earlier, we talked about certain personality types that emerge in the alcoholic, addictive family. Some in the ACOA movement and writers and lecturers in the phenomenon further classify the children of alcoholics into 1) the hero; 2) the scapegoat; 3) the lost child; or 4) the mascot.

Often a hero is an oldest or only child. He or she feels obliged to do something to correct the ills of the family, to heal family pain — often unaware of the depth of his or her own pain. The hero often is quite competent and intelligent, but being perfectionistic,

Patrick J. Brennan

is never quite satisfied with his or her performance. The hero's *goal* is a source of chronic pain and frustration: to straighten out the family. The generous hero often feels tired, frustrated, and depleted in trying to meet the family's needs. The hero always over-extends him/herself. Remember: ACOA's carry these paradigmatic styles with them into all relationships, well into adulthood. Thus, relative to over-extension, heroes run the risk of early burn-out or stress-related illnesses and premature death. The hero is angry, often, at how hard he or she has to try. Like other ACOAs, he/she is often lonely. The hero hides the drinking parent's addiction, family and financial difficulties, and his/her own suppressed feelings.

Scapegoats, on the other hand, are usually *second children.* As has been discovered in the pioneering work of Alfred Adler and Rudolf Dreikurs, children define themselves up against the personalities of their sublings. If heroes are getting attention by being good or achieving in the arena of the family, scapegoats, with similar belonging needs, will go outside of the family for attention.

Feeling rejection from parents, compared to the hero, the scapegoat will seek out a peer group of people with similar bottled up feelings of rejection and frustration. The scapegoat is often defiant, engages in anti-social behavior, gets into trouble at school or with the law. In short, the scapegoat gets attention by being *bad.* Scapegoats, themselves, often use drugs and alcohol. Female scapegoats have a high pregnancy rate early in life. Scapegoats are self-destructive, often engaged in a variety of life destroying activities. Many end up slowly or quickly taking their own lives. The scapegoat's raging anger also covers, loneliness, rejection and hurt. Unfortunately, the largely anti-social peer group he or she associates with is incapable of providing quality relationships or any degree of intimacy. Again, keep in mind, if a scapegoat survives adolescence, he or she carries these dynamics into later adulthood.

A *lost-child* withdraws from family relationships, becomes a loner, retreating into fantasy, TV, media, books, etc. The lost child engages in self-preservation — makes no relational demands, but also receives little or no nurturance. A lost child carries his or her severe introversion and introspection into adulthood. He or she lives a lifetime of feelings of worthlessness, never developing the many levels of potential he or she has. In their lonely, self-enclosed worlds, lost children often turn to eating as a way of nurturance; thus, obesity can be a problem for this sub-group. Because of the extreme loneliness and psychological exile of the lost child, long-term lasting relationships, like friendship or marriage, are almost an impossibility. Because of the almost monastic predisposition of the lost child, he or she has the most potential for developing a spirituality, or spiritual life. In every avenue of life, the lost child will choose a solitary mode of life.

Mascots, finally, are often youngest children. He or

she arrives into an already deteriorated family. As he or she grows, a high level of anxiety builds up in the child. The mascot diffuses this anxiety by playing the role of the clown, or court jester. His or her apparently humorous, but deeply painful, way of life takes the focus off of the alcoholic and family problems.

Mascots have tendencies to develop stress-related physical illnesses. Often diagnosed as hyperactive, they are often medicated. Herein lies another potential within the alcoholic, addictive system for another addiction to take root. Much like the scapegoat can become addicted to street drugs, and the lost child to food, with the mascot there is potential for addiction to prescription drugs. Typically, the mascot appears to be intellectually slow, though that may not be true at all. Rather, because of the raucous, hyperactive role he or she plays, focusing, or staying with something intellectually is a problem. Mascots especially are afraid of looking at the self within.

With all of these typologies, there is the tendency to overlap and bleed into one another.

Recovering

There are various ways to explain the path to recovering for an ACOA. First of all, it is important to highlight the *ing* attached to *recover,* rather than a *y.* In overcoming some of the undertow tendencies, there is not a point of arrival or graduation. Rather than reaching recovery, one is in a constant process of recovering. John Bradshaw, in *Healing the Shame*

PASCHAL JOURNEY

That Blinds You and *Bradshaw On: The Family - A Revolutionary Way of Self Discovery,* speaks of recovering as freeing the imprisoned "child," and breaking through layers of "internalized shame." Still others speak of the need for ACOAs to "become their own parents," since they existentially and psychologically did not have "emotionally present" parents in their growing up. Bradshaw documents some of the compulsions that adult children develop: dieting, work, cleaning, making lists, hoarding, scrupulosity, sexual anxieties, agora-and other phobias, and a variety of psychosomatic disorders. Compulsions that can become addictions are to: alcohol and other drugs, food, sex, excitement, physical abuse and violence, sexual abuse, and sadistic or masochistic behavior. Estimates are as high as 90% of the American population is in some form of addictive — co-dependent web.

As discussed in another chapter, the *will* also plays a great role in the work of John Bradshaw. Bradshaw says there has to be a *willingness* to risk opening one's self to new, therapeutic relationships, and behavior. Co-dependence, he maintains, is a situation of having a *disabled will.* Before that disabled will or intentionality, can be discovered, there is a need to surrender to and through the shame that progressively has buried the self, the child. Frequently, the damaged will, the lost child, the buried self can only begin to be discovered through a new family, of choice, which takes the form of a 12-step group. The gradual progression through the 12 steps, the steps of admitting powerlessness, turning one's diseased will over to God, taking inventory of the self, reaching out and making amends to all whom one has hurt, then trying to help others in a similar process of healing, all gradually edge a person toward, a new *willingness,* or *intentionality* that is oriented toward integrity, intimacy, and growth. To use a distinction made by Dr. Gerald May in *Addiction and Grace,* one's diseased *willfulness,* becomes, through such a process, a more properly disposed *willingness,* or spirit of risk, trust, and serenity.

Thus, recovering is a movement from a *false self* to a *true self.* In terms of the *true self,* religious educator, Maria Harris's reference to the activity of imagination seems especially appropriate: the form was there, is there, waiting to be found. In just the same way, in learning the self was there, is there, and is waiting to be found.

Getting to *Recovering*

It is often only in hindsight that we can see conversion, or, in this instance, re-covering has taken, is taking place. The twelve step process of Alcoholics Anonymous, Al-ateen, Adult Children of Alcoholics, and other twelve-step processes seems to be the best environment for getting the process started. Adult children of addicted parents need:

- an environment of safety;
- understanding peers;
- companions who communicate genuine acceptance;

126

- often the first experience of emotional bonding;
- a re-education of their feelings;
- a renewed sense of play;
- an opportunity to grieve lost life, lost youth;
- a commitment to recovery work;
- people to "faith with";
- understanding others who also know how to confront when that is needed;
- opportunities to, in effect, come out of hiding.

Why Bother?

What is the relevance of all this for the ordinary reader? Well, as the previous statistics indicate, few of us are not in some way ourselves addicted or co-dependent, or know someone who is. I am increasingly surprised by the prevalence of substance or process addictions and co-dependency syndromes in individual lives, relationships, and organizations — like businesses or the Church. Specific to alcohol:

- remember again the high suicide rate among the children of alcoholism;
- physical, sexual, and emotional abuse are present in most alcoholic homes;
- alcoholism and other addictions, occur in families; there is opinion that this is the result of learning; others say it is a matter of genetic influence; others contend it is a result of both;
- the phenomenon of children of alcoholics marrying alcoholics is a recurrent one

Patrick J. Brennan

In a "society that has become an addict," we all would do well to learn more about the dynamics of addiction and co-dependency.

Journal Questions for Individuals and Small Groups

1) What is the quality of your own spiritual program? Are you doing things, not doing things, that keep you in daily conscious contact with God and others?

2) Have addictions influenced your life in any way? How? In the lives of people you know? How? Spend quiet time in prayer, seeking healing for yourself and/or others.

3) Writer Keith Miller says that while organized religions continue to diminish in numbers, twelve-step programs are abounding. Why is this true?

4) How could the church, which relates to many people in an institutionalized way, become more a community of healing, similar to 12 step groups? Guide the reflection discussion toward your own or your group's lived experience of Church, in the local parish.

Chapter Eleven

Commitment: <u>Always?</u>

A SONG of several years ago poignantly asked "Does anyone stay together anymore?" The ballad was a reflection of the apparent reluctance of many young people to make long-term commitments to each other in marriage and other relationships, the over 50% divorce rate among first time marriages, and the 60% divorce rate in second marriages. I would not want to hang "commitment reluctance" just on the young adult population. I am recurrently disturbed at the large number of couples in their 30's, 40's, and 50's who appear in the counseling office, apparently unable to live any longer with each other.

Juxtaposed in my mind with the above is the image of John, a friend of mine who recently died of cancer. Some days before his death, he told me of a nightly practice of his. Every night, he said, in the presence of God, he made an act of re-commitment to his wife, vowing eternal love to her again and again — daily. At his funeral, I said that John was certainly cut from a different fabric than that which makes up the culture today.

A Mirror Image

There are many reasons for marriages falling apart. Perhaps one general one is that some of the malaise of the culture has begun to bleed into our personal and interpersonal lives. *Privatism* and *individualism* are words that characterize our society. The heavily relational tone of earlier decades of America has been replaced by excessive self-focus. Even magazine titles reflect the cultural shifts that we have experienced. *Life* has been bumped by *People,* which is in competition with *US,* which now has a competitor in *Self.* People no longer enter relationships with a concern for the relationship, but rather their self-interest or well-being in the context of the relationship. Some would call this a healthy development, with more people invested in self-actualization. Others, myself included, feel that true self-actualization is only had through self transcendence, or giving one's self to someone or others. Thus, today's relationships are a mirror image of what is going on in society — the relational bond is never as important as self-gratification. We examine in this chapter some of the subtle undertows that are present in today's marriages or attempts at intimate relationships.

Role and Rule Change

It is inevitable that in a relationship, things will change over the passage of time. A disgruntled husband recently sat down across the office from me and his wife of fifteen years. His complaint was that his wife "was not the same woman he had married." This sounded rather obvious to me. People who expect a relationship to remain the same are either awfully naive, or controlling, or both. Relationships are constituted by explicit or implicit rules; and implicit or explicit role playing.

Rules is a general term for a number of should's, ought's, have to's, and must's that develop between the partners in a relationship. *Roles* speak of the part(s) we play in the drama of a relationship: worker, mother, father, friend, superior, inferior, the giver, the taker, etc. It is impossible to relate to someone without these rules and roles evolving. Often rules and roles are implicit, that is, they are not talked about too much.

Usually a relationship coasts along until one or both parties alters either the rules or the roles or both. Again, because of the implicit nature of roles and rules, little communication has taken place about them or does take place about them. But one or both parties in the relationship are angry because some sort of disequilibrium has been created. The husband that I spoke of above described his wife as "not the same," specifically "no fun anymore." He critiqued her physical appearance, mentioning that the weight she put on since the advent of their three children was a turn-off to him. Though his tone of voice was demeaning, he actually was crying for help. He felt as though he had lost his best friend and romantic interest. She, in turn, was protesting with hurt. Didn't he realize that her apparent inability to have fun, and weight gain were direct results of having three children in quick succession, that she has indeed become "super mom." The years of marriage have dramatically changed the roles and rules these two play with each other. The communication begun in counseling has begun to drain off some of the anger that has developed between the both of them. They are becoming aware that they both need to change to accommodate the changing roles and rules brought on by the passage of time. Before the counseling, however, he was not sure whether he wanted to continue in the relationship. He had been seriously contemplating divorce.

Non-Sexual Infidelity

Typically men have been identified as the ones more in love with their jobs than with their spouses. Recently I have experienced several couples where the shoe was on the other foot — namely women, who, after having raised children, have gone to work. In re-entering the work force they have grown tremendously enamored with the self esteem that they gain from work. This in itself has been good for these women. But in several cases, one in particular, the job has taken on spousal qualities. The amount of time, psychic energy, and quality of relating that should be given to marriage and family is being given to work. In fact, in this one instance, work relationships have taken on a new familial tone. The husband has been discarded, first emotionally, and now legally. The wife protests she has outgrown the marriage, or perhaps it was a mistake to begin with. She wants a divorce. The husband genuinely feels blind-sided. Where has all this disdain for the relationship come from? How can she want out of the marriage so quickly?

In the case I am referring to, a woman has become infatuated with her job, and allowed her primary responsibility to her spouse and children to erode. Though she claims not to have slept with or been sexually involved with anyone, she has nonetheless been unfaithful to spouse and the children. Infidelity need not involve genital sexual experiences. Infidelity in a relationship consists of either of the partners giving more of his or her heart to someone or something other than one's primary relationships. One of my rules of thumb in counseling is that rather sudden unexplainable behavior usually has to do with drug or alcohol abuse, or infidelity. So often in a marriage or dating relationship it is infidelity, or giving one's heart to someone or something else. I have seen marriages in which spouses have been unfaithful to each other around sports, hobbies, Church activities, work, and on and on.

It is not that sports, job, hobbies, Church activities, etc. are bad things. Rather, they have to be re-viewed and placed in proper perspective. Key to breaking through such non-sexual infidelity is the ability to negotiate — each party in a relationship, after discernment and discussion, trying to change the self to better relate to the other, to contribute more to the stability of the relationship. Negotiation is difficult for people raised in a culture that advocates self-actualization to a fault, that prizes winning and the consequent parallel: that there must be losers.

Patrick J. Brennan

The Affair

Some relationships have suffered damage from an actual emotional, physical infidelity. There is no one reason for an affair: they can be expressions of immaturity, revenge, indiscretion, unfulfilled needs, etc. But I have begun to sense another avenue of causality recently in this age of me-ism. I think some, *at least some people,* become involved with a third party because of a narcissistic urge to avoid merging more intimately with their current partner. For example, to continue with a mid-life spouse or partner in the ongoing journey of intimacy, with some of the unique pains of mid-life and aging certainly is not as immediately gratifying as going off with another perhaps younger, more attractive person, someone who perhaps activates some repressed or forgotten youthfulness in the one who is straying. Thus, sexual infidelity is often not the first real discovery of intimacy as it is often supposed to be. It is rather often a *flight from intimacy,* back toward self gratification, the use of another person for another.

Staying with and growing with someone can be a frightening prospect for some people. While it holds some real rewards, namely genuine communion, and oneness, there is also built into commitment genuine self emptying for, and to, another person. Self-sacrificial love, a theme that I write about and talk about frequently, is a great threat to today's self-actualizing society.

PASCHAL JOURNEY

I saw self-sacrificial love ritualized beautifully recently at a wedding I was part of. The priest-witness to the vows did not allow the couple to speak their vows to each other at the front of the sanctuary, as is the custom in so many churches. Rather, he called them more deeply into the sanctuary and had them stand beneath the cross in the sanctuary. He pointed out that the crucifix was a "glorified cross." As Christ knew the victory and glory of resurrection, so also people in love know the glory of love. But he maintained that the glory of love is always joined to woundedness for and often because of the other. When Paul and others admonish us to take up the cross, they are not asking us to take on any additional neurotic self-punishment. No, they are inviting us to love with the same kind of love Jesus had on the cross.

Again, an affair often can be an escape from the deeper levels of intimacy, an escape from self sacrificial love, an escape from the love of the cross.

Divorce or Separation as a Ritual of Burial

I have known people who have separated from another as a ritual of having gone through a stage process of growth and self awareness. Perhaps such a stage has involved getting in touch with clusters of pain, neurosis, or moral evil in one's life, and having to wrestle with purging one's self of it. Sometimes leaving behind a cluster of pain, neurosis, hurt, or sin necessitates breaking out of some toxic relationships. Getting out of co-dependent relationships, for exam-

135

ple is a ritual of burying past pain, that is perhaps healthy.

Sometimes, however, leaving a relationship is a ritual not of growth, but a burial of feelings, memories, or guilt. And those kinds of things refuse to be buried. People carry their ghosts around with them. You cannot bury hurt. Emotions, like water, will always rise to their own natural level. I have known men and women who have left another well-meaning, committed, healthy partner as a ritual of their having grown out of something. Often I fear growth has not taken place at all. Rather someone is trying to *bury* a painful part of his or her past by leaving another person. The abandoned person, feeling shocked in this situation, often does not understand the dynamics of what has happened at all. The departing partner really does not understand what he or she is doing either, and therefore cannot explain it. The abandoned spouse or partner can only feel embittered, confused and victimized. Other people are not stages on which we can enact our rights of passage; neither are they sacrificial lambs, to be offered on the altar of narcissism and self-actualizing.

The Stagnant Relationship or Marriage

Perhaps the most insidious of dying relationships is what is called in marriage counseling: "the stable, unsatisfactory" relationship. In this relationship or marriage, neither partner is truly happy or gratified by the nature of the relationship, but they remain in

136

it. They remain in it because it is easier than trying to terminate it or, better yet, working at it, fixing it, or improving it. Minister-writer-lecturer, Ken Potts, a pastoral psychotherapist from the Chicago area, said recently in a newspaper article that marriage (or, I would submit, relationships in general) do either of two things — they grow or they die. Often death is a result, Potts wrote of intra-psychic monologues in the partners' minds that sound something like this: "Don't rock the boat . . . leave well enough alone . . . let it ride . . ." Such verbiage is often used, as noted previously, to bury something, in this case, dissatisfaction in the relationship. It is tremendously sad to witness a slowly dying relationship, wherein two people know things are not going well, but they leave things untouched. Often such relationships could begin again to bear fruit, to grow, if as in previous examples, people sit down with each other to communicate, negotiate, encourage, and challenge.

Often fear keeps people from working on their slowly eroding relationships. One can fear that bringing up dissatisfaction will lead to ultimate rejection by the other. Others of us fear that any critique, criticism or negative feedback is a proof positive that we are unloveable, unacceptable people. In other words, we fear abandonment if we communicate or we fear condemnation if we are critiqued. Consequently people keep their mouths shut. The process of erosion continues to diminish the shore line of love and commitment. People can be emotionally divorced,

Patrick J. Brennan

while still in a relationship to and present with another, and while still being married to another.

The relationship, however, is a life-long reproduction of *The Night of the Living Dead* and the sad thing is that the courage to communicate could break through the stagnation quite easily.

Gender Differences and Relationships

The least complicated difference between men and women to understand is the physical difference. Two more complicated realities are the different processes of socialization that males and females experience, resulting in markedly different inner worlds; and the fact that men and women rarely go through emotional stages at the same chronological time. Gail Sheehy wrote on the latter years ago. More recently Carol Gilligan and others have written and spoken about the different interior landscapes of the female and male psyches. Alfred Adler said it first: The great revolution awaiting us is the sexes' understanding and relating to each other better.

Greater empathy needs to be practiced by both of the sexes in trying to understand each other's mysterious inner worlds: what is it like to be male in this society; what is it like to be female in this society? If we, as males and females, really tried to get a feel for each other's shoes, we would be making great strides in improving relationships. Similarly, if we learned to wait for a member of the opposite sex to go through a stage, one perhaps we have already accomplished or one still

138

awaiting us, there would be much less emotional divorce in our culture.

Conclusion

We explored many dimensions of how relationships — especially marriages — come unglued and fall apart. The importance of this brief study is in the positive underpinning beneath it all. We have been made for fidelity and indissolubility in relationships. "Love never ends," says Paul in *1 Corinthians.* I feel it is important to confront and name some of the demons in our culture and in our psyches, which are products of the culture, which keep us from faithful, indissoluble relationships. Having named them, we then can do something about them.

Journal Questions for Individuals and Small Groups

1) What is the oldest, most healthy relationship that you have? What has made it so long-lasting and healthy?

2) Are there any things that you are burying rather than communicating to someone important in your life?

3) Do you or the group agree, with the importance of gender differences — why or why not?

4) Reflect on or discuss non-sexual infidelity. What are the seductive forces that rob us of healthy relationships?

Chapter Twelve

Anxiety Revisited

". . . They that hope in the Lord will renew their strength; they will soar as with eagles' wings; they will run and not grow weary, walk and not grow faint. . . . I am the Lord your God, who grasps your right hand. It is I who say to you 'Fear not, I will help you.'" — *Isaiah 40: 31; 41-13.*

I WROTE a book on a spiritual response to stress and anxiety several years ago entitled *Spirituality for An Anxious Age.* Subtitled "Into Your Hands . . .", the book documents some classical theories concerning the origins of anxiety, plus my own gradual transformation that led me to see much anxiety as being at root a trust, or spirituality problem. Consider how humbling it is, to be a writer and lecturer on the topic of stress and anxiety, and to have had the following experience.

Recently, for a couple of weeks in a row, I did not feel well — vague feelings of discomfort, stomach distress, subtle chest pains, but just enough to get a 43-year-old a little worried. I am borderline "Christian Scientist" when it comes to doctors, but nonetheless, I felt a visit this time might be warranted.

PASCHAL JOURNEY

Actually I saw him a couple of times and went through several tests before he delivered his diagnosis.

"You're under too much stress!"

"What?"

"The problem here is stress!"

I was disappointed. After working up enough courage to come to the doctor, couldn't he come up with something more dramatic than stress.

I went on, "Well, doctor, what do you recommend?"

The doctor pondered for a moment. "Go home and recommit your life to Christ."

I know my doctor is a Catholic, but this prescription seemed a bit naive. Seriously, I felt quite humbled. Not only had I apparently lost psychological congruency with, or awareness of myself as a psychotherapist; as a priest, I also seemed to have lost touch with the connection between communion with God and inner peace. "Go re-commit your life to Christ," suggested to me that while Jesus might have been grasping for me, inviting me, simply there for me, I was not responding to his invitation. Oh, I was praying, worshipping, etc., but perhaps it was not as heartfelt as it could or should have been. I had to go home, searching again for the peace only God and a spiritual program can bring.

My doctor's advice reminded me of a story I read recently regarding an author, Arthur Gordon, whose personal story of transformation, "The Turn of the Tide," is recounted in Stephen Covey's excellent book

Patrick J. Brennan

The Seven Habits of Highly Effective People. Gordon also, feeling ill-at-ease, and washed out, went to a medical doctor for help. Finding nothing wrong with him, the doctor asked Gordon if he would take the next day off and follow his instructions for one day. The author responded yes. The doctor then said the day would have to be spent in the place he felt the happiest as a child. Thus, Arthur Gordon went to the beach the following day, with written prescriptions from the doctor, to be opened at nine, twelve, three and six o'clock.

The doctor's nine o'clock prescription read: "Listen carefully." For the next three hours, Gordon was reminded how noisy his life had become, and how he needed to rekindle a quiet, listening spirit for the times he was alone and with others. The noon prescription was "Reach back," an admonition to re-call and make present again memories of happy times. The three o'clock prescription was a bit more challenging: "Examine your motives." Gordon was challenged to see that some of his earlier, more purified motivation had gone awry. The six o'clock prescription was "write your worries on the sand." He did so and walked away, knowing eventually the tide would wash away what he had written. Both Arthur Gordon and Stephen Covey enflesh what my doctor was hinting at. Stress and consequent psychosomatic disorders can be a result of forgetting to listen, to remember, to center on the best motives, and turning over or surrendering worries.

PASCHAL JOURNEY

Gordon, Covey, and my doctor made me retrieve, but also become convinced anew of some of the core convictions in some of my early writing, like *Spirituality for An Anxious Age.* Central to that material were the following common sense suggestions, which are nonetheless difficult in their simplicity.

1) *Listen to yourself:* A great deal of the anxiety or stress that we feel, be it intra-psychic or psychosomatic, is really symptomatic of repressed feelings, or other parts of our lives either not going well, or not being well integrated or assimilated. We need to listen (and look) beyond the often painful symptoms to conflicts or unprocessed material underneath the symptoms.

2) *Gain Insight:* Attending to, listening to the self provides insight into anxiety's or stress's etiology or causality. As we will discuss later, usually most stress or anxiety is a result of one or more of the following:

   a) — a learned response to life;
   b) — the stress filled culture that we live in;
   c) — certain stress producing situations we find ourselves in or people that we find ourselves with;
   d) — stages of adulthood and the trauma that they sometimes bring with them;
   e) — a physical pre-disposition toward, or high sensitization to certain stimuli that almost

automatically trigger the brain-body's alert or warning system;

f) — busyness addiction: the felt experience of overload, burn-out, or inability to continue to deliver on multiple demands;

g) — a spiritual problem: a forgetting, or not yet having awakened to the unconditional love that calms fear, the love that Isaiah speaks of in the opening Scripture passage. Jesus speaks of this love in *Matthew 11:* "Come to me, all you who are weary and find life burdensome, and I will refresh you . . . Your souls will find rest."

Jesuit writer William O'Malley, a frequent contributor to *America* magazine wrote recently that one of the problems with American consumer culture is that so many of us forget we are *souls, spirits,* seeking meaning, purpose, and the kind of interior rest that only God can provide.

3) *Make Decisions.* Growth takes place, in this case an easing of anxiety and stress, by deciding on some therapeutic goals for one's self. For example, if the anxiety has been traced in steps 1 and 2 to any one or a synthesis of "a through g", then a spiritual-emotional pilgrim can set some reasonable goals as to how to get at those causes, turn some of them around, or transfer negative energy into positive energy. The decisions made should be simple, the goals reasonable and reach-

able. This stage harkens back to our section on the importance of *will* and *will power*. The making and execution of decisions needs the energy of will to become operative.

Will, in turn, needs to be supported by *intellect, emotions,* and *imagination.* Decisions and therapeutic goals will undoubtedly not always be perfectly achieved. People trying to do "deliberative living" as Walt Whitman called it, need to give themselves room, or the courage to be imperfect. For example, I might see the root cause of fear or anxiety in my life to be "busyness addiction." I might make a decision, and set a goal to build 20 minutes of creative alone time in my daily life. There may be a day or series of days when circumstances do not permit me to use that time as I want to. The worst scenario is to throw in the towel and give up on the therapeutic practice. Rather, I need to learn from the setback, become aware of all the days ahead that will afford me the opportunity for those 20 minutes of meditation, and then start again.

4) *Taking action.* Behavior change is key to all psychological, spiritual, or relational growth. The old line, "You are what you eat" can be expanded to "You are what you do, and what you do repetitively." If we were always to act on our feelings, many of us would not get out of bed in the morning. Emotions or feelings are gasoline in the car,

Patrick J. Brennan

the foot on or off the pedal determines how the gasoline will be used. Taking action or behavior change is the engine, pulling the train of our emotions, decisions, will, and imagination. Often "acting as if" is necessary; only later do those more numinous parts of ourselves catch up with our behavior. I am convinced that frequently therapy is not effective or as effective as it could be because therapists do not make deliberate attempts with clients to behavioralize their insights, decisions, and goals in, small manageable pieces.

5) *Practice:* Perhaps this positively reiterates the principle of not giving in to failures or setbacks. It amazes me that we can spend a good part of our lifetime practicing golf swings, racquetball techniques, or career abilities, yet we give so little of that slow, plodding, deliberate, repetitive effort to practicing psycho-spiritual or relational growth. As 1-4 emerges as truth for us we must practice being "new beings."

In all of this, there is or will be no growth without a willingness to experience some discomfort. I am not speaking here of an imposed Catholic — neurotic pain that we needlessly inflict on ourselves. Much of what passed itself off as spirituality in previous years was in fact sado-masochism. I am speaking of a healthy pain or discomfort that one is willing to take on for greater good of health, growth, and love.

In a culture of immediate gratification and anesthesization of discomfort, the struggle involved in growth is often a price people are unwilling to pay.

6) *Spiritual Program.* The notion of a spiritual program is borrowed from the language and vision of twelve-step programs. Stephen Covey (*The Seven Habits of Highly Effective People*) calls the same phenomenon *Sharpening the Saw.* Covey feels that scheduled into everyone's time management sheets (which he prefers to the notion of an appointment book) ought to be "sharpening the saw time." This time ought to be used to sharpen or renew the self. Covey feels that what I call "spiritual program time" ought to be used for four purposes, in what ever prioritization a person feels is necessary in a given week or period of time. The four goals or ends are: mental renewal (through reading, etc.), physical renewal (through diet, exercise, etc.), social renewal (through positive, life-giving relationship time), and spiritual renewal (through meditation, or whatever technique fits a given personality).

William Glasser had different terms for this some years ago when he spoke of replacing negative addictions with positive addictions. He specifically highlighted daily physical exercise and meditation as important stages of a positive addiction process. In a turn of phrase, addiction expert Diane Fassel speaks of "transforming a process of negative addiction into living a (healthy) process."

In strict twelve-step ideology, a spiritual program cannot be imposed. One needs to be helped to find what works for him or her, in terms of finding one self's relative inner peace, and placing the self in daily conscious contact with the Higher Power (God). For example, through personality testing, namely the Meyers-Briggs test, which is rooted in a Jungian vision of life, I found that I have an introverted personality type. In the Jungian-Meyers-Briggs view, introvert or extrovert is neither good nor bad. Introverts need to go within themselves for reenergizing. Extraverts usually do it via social interaction, which is only another depletion of energy for introverts. This does not mean that introverts cannot be good with people, nor that extraverts are lacking in interior depth. It means simply different personalities re-fuel in different ways.

I have found that a spiritual program that works for me involves: 1) at least 20 minutes of silence and meditation per day; 2) daily jogging and other exercise; 3) reading; 4) journaling; 5) frequent Eucharist. I try to "work this process" rather than allow life to live me. As I said at the beginning of this section, often when I begin to slide in this program-process — or in the other six dimensions of emotional growth that I have highlighted, it is then the symptoms of anxiety, fear, and stress begin to re-appear.

Stress vs. Panic

At this point, it might be helpful to distinguish between the stress some ordinary people may feel, and the extreme panic other people experience who are usually called "agoraphobics." I believe that everything that I have said so far applies, in fact, to both groups. In others words, stress *and* panic can result from: 1) not listening to one's self; 2) a lack of insight into one's vision and convictions; 3) not setting therapeutic goals, or making willful, healthy decisions; 4) not taking therapeutic action in one's life; 5) not practicing healthy living patterns; 6) not developing and living a wholistic spiritual program; or 7) the general causes of a stressful, anxious approach to life; a) faulty learning; b) the culture we live in; c) real life stress-producing people or situations; d) a developmental stage that carries with it a certain amount of trauma; e) a psycho-physical predisposition; f) busyness addiction; g) not having had a conversion or spiritual awakening to the God of Jesus.

In other words, the above patterns fit both stress and panic syndromes. But stress and panic differ in terms of intensity and also causality. Let us look at stress first.

Stress

Stress seems to flow most clearly from the above dynamics and is the most manageable. People who

149

Patrick J. Brennan

have allowed themselves to become stress-filled usually exhibit all or some of the following:

1) fatigue: never feeling sufficiently rested;
2) a growing pattern of being argumentative;
3) impatience and intolerance toward others' imperfections;
4) difficulty in relaxing;
5) pressure feeling because of job or relationships;
6) time constraints;
7) not enough time for primary relationships and consequent guilt;
8) a growing aversion to social gatherings;
9) a certain amount of mental confusion that often involves absentmindedness or forgetfulness;
10) frequent feeling of irritability;
11) attempts to do more than one thing at the same time;
12) feelings of competition — sometimes with one's self and some past achievement

Other psychosomatic symptoms could be listed to fill pages. Among them are: racing heart or pseudo heart attack pain, muscle twitches and tension, sweating, headaches, gastrointestinal difficulties, trembling, cardiovascular symptoms like heightened blood pressure, diffuse and undefined anxiety feelings, abuse of alcohol and its consequent after effects, feelings of detachment or a felt sense of unreality.

This of course is only a survey consideration of generalized stress syndrome. I believe, however, that most

PASCHAL JOURNEY

stress is symptomatic of something(s) else and can be readily managed via the "listen, gain insight, make decisions, take action, practice, develop a spiritual program strategy or discipline.

Panic

A young man, first a counselee, now a good friend of mine, and I sat at dinner recently. He is a successful businessman, married to a wonderful wife. A priest-therapist-evangelist, I am fairly effective. We both shared wonder that either of us had gotten as far as we have, because we both have suffered from agoraphobia and concomitant panic attacks. Agoraphobia is generally a fear of leaving a psychological home base, of being immersed in the network of people and experience called life. Often certain stimuli gain the power to cause panic attacks — which are a conglomerate of many of the symptoms of stress previously mentioned, happening all at once. Panic attacks are dreadfully painful experiences of feeling the loss of one's emotions and body.

In *Spirituality for An Anxious Age,* I documented how I am working on managing panic in my life. More recently I became acquainted with an organization dedicated to self-help groups for agoraphobics. Even more recently, I had the pleasure of addressing one such group. There was something very releasing in speaking to a group, not as Pat Brennan — the expert, but rather Pat Brennan in a "Damien the Leper posture." I began with the words "We agoraphobics."

151

Patrick J. Brennan

The name of the organization is *Agoraphobics in Motion,* or *A.I.M.*

A.I.M. has groups proliferating widely now. *A.I.M.* groups try to teach phobics ten rules to live by. These rules are similar to wisdom found in *Spirituality For An Anxious Age* and other works by Claire Weekes and Dr. David Sheehan.

1) Realize feelings are an exaggeration of normal bodily reactions to stress.
2) These feelings are not life threatening or harmful; nothing serious can come from them.
3) Stop fueling these feelings with further panic-ridden thoughts and feelings — I call this the secondary fear, or fear of being afraid syndrome.
4) Attend to what is going on in your body when an attack is coming or has come.
5) Wait — don't fight or take flight. Fear and panic will rather quickly pass. To fight or take flight prolongs and exacerbates it.
6) Notice how quickly when you deliberately slow everything down, or let the fear pass, the fear fades.
7) Every attack is an opportunity to learn or practice.
8) Always rejoice in the progress you are making (and I would add — resolve never to give in to the self-pity that would result in severe backsliding).

9) Build on small accomplishments — after reaching one plateau of growth, decide about what the next small victory should be. It can be as small as exposing yourself briefly to some new stimuli that evokes fear, that you might further desensitize yourself.

10) Move slowly, in an easy, relaxed manner. (Phobics are usually obsessive compulsives who want to control the rapid progression of their recovery. I tell clients "if it took this long to get you this way, it is going to take a while to turn things around!")

Mary Ann Miller is the foundress of A.I.M. In advertising the group process, her materials outline what she has found to be the key pieces to recovery. I would like to re-iterate no one is ever totally *recovered,* but is *recovering.* Ms. Miller's principles are as follows:

1) Belief that recovery is possible, is crucial. (Notice again, the importance of will, decision, choice.)

2) Relaxation and Meditation (Notice again, the spiritual roots of anxiety.)

3) Self Talk — listen to and eliminate negative messages to yourself (A.A. calls such messages "stinkin' thinkin')

4) Affirmations — This is simply the flipping around of negative images, that is, to flood one's mind with positive images. (Either using prayerful rehearsal or prayerful meditative exercises,

Patrick J. Brennan

one can place one's self in the typical anxiety-producing setting, but rather, rehearse being and doing in the scene with a spirit of peace and trust.)

5) *Books:* In Adlerian training, we use the technical term of *bibliotherapy,* or the use of good self-help books that help a person to imagine a new *self.* (Please take note in 2, 3, 4, and 5 on the centrality of the imagination in creating a new self and self image. I write more extensively on the power of the imagination in my book, *Re-Imagining the Parish* (Crossroads — Continuum: 1990)

6) *Goal-Setting:* Ms. Miller re-iterates the previously mentioned importance of decisions, goals, and practicing.

7) *Exposure.* This needs to be highlighted. Weeks and others have written extensively on the need to step by step, gradually expose one's self to the stimuli that evokes fear. Gradually there is a de-sensitization to the stimuli. Phobic people may be sensitive people, but they are even more sensitized. Almost like allergy-prone people, they will only diminish their over-reaction to something by gradual doses of or exposure to the aggravating situation. I'll say more on this later when I speak on paradoxical intention.

8) *Telephone:* Phobics, again, are home-based type people. They like "terra firma." To be able to

connect with similarly struggling people via phone is a source of great support.

9) *Group meetings:* Further support is offered in group relationships, providing struggling people with feelings of acceptance, belonging, and bonding.

10) *Spiritual Program:* Ms. Miller would here concur with what we have discussed earlier.

Three Special Issues:
Intention, Medication, and Alcohol Abuse

1) Paradoxical Intention

Dr. Frank Dattilo, writing in the *Journal of Counseling and Development* in October, 1987 (Vol. 66) estimated the number of people in the United States suffering from panic attacks to be between 4 and 10 million. Dattilo's article was entitled "The Use of Paradoxical Intention in the Treatment of Panic Attacks." Actually, we need first to give credit where credit is due. The first person that I know of, who wrote years ago on paradoxical intention was Victor Frankl in *Man's Search for Meaning* and later in *Logotherapy.* The concept of paradoxical intention is difficult to explain to people for it is the acceptance of discomfort and desensitization to the maximum. As Frankl taught years ago, and Dattilo writes about now much more scientifically, the essence of paradoxical intention is to will the fear-producing situation, or an actual panic attack, to happen. The insight behind paradoxical intention is that if a person can muster up enough courage to say to the fear producing event "Come on! Enter my life. Yes, I fear you, but you will not control me." In making such a frontal assault, a paradoxical invitation, one begins to rob the fear-producer of its power. Frankl used to say it robs the sails of wind.

I personally have found and find paradoxical intention very helpful in recovery from phobia. Because faith is a deeply rooted reality in my life, I have actually engaged in paradoxically intentioned prayer, wherein I pray for the feared reality to enter my life. When I tell people this in counseling or lectures, they think I am crazy. The good news is: it works. The bottom line is pragmatic.

Gallati wrote: ". . . actual exposure to the feared situation (known as "flooding") and the use of the paradoxical intent are the key to reducing symptoms" (p. 103).

2) Medication

For some whose panic seems to be deeply wedded to chemistry and physiology and for those who need a temporary crutch to reduce anxiety so that courage may be regained, medication may be needed. Such a course of action must only be done via consultation with psychiatrists currently familiar with psycho-pharmacology. Most drugs have positive effects but also some debilitating side effects. Therefore, unless absolutely necessary, the use of anxiety-reducing drugs, or anxiolytics as they are popularly known, should involve a supervised "easing away from" period, when the phobic is deemed ready.

Let us first try to understand how general stress or extreme panic happens neurologically and in the brain's functioning and chemistry. The brain, like the rest of the body is made up of cells. A neuron is a nerve cell, that contains the information processing and transmitting elements of the nervous system. Neurons are connected to each other via synapses or connectors. Every neuron has a kind of stem called an axon, that carries a substance called "transmitter substance," to the synapse that connects it to another neuron. This substance, in a sense, spills through the synapse to the next neuron, activating receptors on the next neuron. The progression goes on like so many folding cards, or activated lights. In feelings of fear or panic, perception affects certain neurons in the brain that lead to this fight or flight activation. It is all electrical and chemical, though again affected by perception and learning and goes on quite unconsciously and automatically in the brain.

The effect of the major tranquilizing drugs is to inhibit or shut down the firing of the neurons involved in that part of the brain associated with panic or fear. Many hypothesize that the thalamus and hypothalamus are the parts of the brain most affected. For the reader's information, the major, current anoxiolytics are:

Patrick J. Brennan

- Librium
- Valium
- Serax
- Tranxene
- Centrax
- Xanax
- Paxipam
- Ativan
- and Buspar — which is an anti-depressant which also functions as an anxiolytic

I can only caution that any such drug usage should be done in extreme circumstances, under the advice and supervision of a psychiatrist. Otherwise we may have another problem besides anxiety: addiction.

3) Alcohol Abuse

Research shows that many with either generalized stress or panic disorders turn to alcohol for relief. Unfortunately, alcohol does not produce the desired effects. If taken in moderation, alcohol can be a pleasant, mild sedative, best joined to food intake. But in cases of abuse where it replaces one's natural caloric intake, and wherein addiction begins to set in, the neurons again are affected. The centers of the brain responding to alcohol stimulation begin to crave more and more. Alcohol abuse often produces a biochemical neurological quagmire equivalent to *hypoglycemia* with light-headedness apprehension. In other words, what the drinker is trying to get rid of, he or she makes worse through alcohol abuse. Alcohol rattles the nervous system worse than it originally was. As this condition worsens, one may turn to the anxiolytics to relieve the extreme anxiety now present. Now we have 3 free-standing, but also related syndromes to treat:

158

stress or panic, alcohol abuse, and drug abuse. The quest then becomes to choose which of the pathologies to address first, or which is the most toxic.

The six simple steps of listening to self, gaining insights, making decisions, taking action, practicing, and developing a spiritual program certainly seems the more natural and human way to go in trying to temper stress or anxiety.

Journal Questions for Individuals and Small Groups

1) Which of the six main steps (beginning with listening to self) do you need to practice to have a healthier lifestyle?

2) What are your fears? What are sources of stress? To what degree do you panic? How can you better manage?

3) How can we as a group help each other, like the A.I.M. members, to lead lives of greater peace?

4) Where did you hear yourself being talked about in the chapter? What changes do you want to make? What would such changes look like in behavior?

Chapter Thirteen

An Anniversary

". . . Do this in memory of me . . ." Luke 22:19.

3:30 PM

IT IS Friday, 3:30 in the afternoon, 1990. Last year, on this date, August 24, my mother and then my cousin called me to come to the hospital to see my father. My mother was unaware of the gravity of the situation; my cousin was there with my father in the hospital in yet another of a series of acute congestive heart failure episodes. I quickly left my office and hurried to Chicago's south side, to Christ Hospital.

It was hard to know what to feel or what to pray for anymore. August 24 really began with August 9, my father's 80th birthday. I was called to the hospital that morning, for he had suffered his third heart attack and heart failure episode in one year. I guess I was even more apprehensive on August 9; for on the occasion of heart attack number two, the previous spring, the doctor had told me that he would never survive another such episode. His lungs and muscles were beyond repair or therapy. I asked his heretofore extremely positive nurse: "Is he dying?" She replied, "I think so."

160

PASCHAL JOURNEY

7:00 PM

My mother arrived with my Aunt Kate, the real grandmother figure in our family. This was unannounced and not prepared for. I had tried to protect my mother from any symbols or signs of death, but she was not to be discouraged. She penetrated all protective lines, and upon arrival, marched with determination to my father's intensive care unit.

"Hey, you," she said with authority.

For the first time in hours, he opened his eyes. He responded to her voice, alone. None of us in the last hours, in the last day, had been able to rouse much attention from him.

"Body of Christ," he replied.

My mother is an auxiliary minister of communion. As part of her ministry, she held communion services in their home, for herself and my father. In fact her history in the ministry is an interesting one. Some three years before my father's acute problems, she fell victim to congestive heart failure — only a symptom of a deeper pathology — mitrostenosis, a chronic disease affecting the mitral valve of the heart. In the aftermath of her hospitalization, she fell into a deep depression, and lost her belief in the power of prayer. I asked her during this depressed period to get on her knees and pray with me. As I led her in prayer, I noticed her face, her countenance change. Depression seemed to instantaneously change to hope. I became convinced about how important faith and prayer were and are to physical and emotional healing. After this incident I invited her to consider making Eucharistic devotion a daily part of her prayer life with my father.

So, daily my mother had been giving my father communion. One of the regular communication exchanges between the both of them was "Body of Christ," and "Amen." In this his own personal health crisis, my father was articulating who my mother had been and was to him, a minister of the healing, presence, and Spirit of Christ.

In hindsight, I envy the position that my mother held. For I was in another one. I was the legally responsible one, the one that signed or did not sign for life support, the one who was asked whether he should be resuscitated or not. In fact for the past ten years, I had been caretaker of both my mother and father.

During the hours of 7-9 pm, I recurrently replaced the oxygen mask on my father's face. He consistently responded by taking it off, looking at me, then firmly declaring "I'm dead." Some might find this morbid but it is true. It was almost as if he were declaring to me that he had decided to co-operate with nature, with God — that he was voluntarily passing to the other side of this life. It was almost as if he wanted permission to go, to die.

I sent my mother home, with others who had gathered. At 9:30 pm my brother and I went to a restaurant across the street to get something to eat. We both realized that we were in the final scene of my father's

162

life. We both knew that he was dying. I told my brother that the neurologist reported to me that my father was experiencing strange brain activity. In addition to all of his other problems, he probably was having mini-strokes.

So that all of us might get a few hours sleep, I ordered that my father be minimally restrained overnight. He was thrashing about pulling off the oxygen mask. I often regret not having stayed with him that night.

Dawn, August 25, '89

My brother and I met at the hospital at about 9 in the morning. My father was non-responsive, offering only a minimal squeeze to my hand in recognition of my presence. He was sweating profusely; his breathing was in short, panting spurts. He stared straight ahead. Nonetheless, the doctors and staff reassured me that the last dialysis treatment was successful in lowering the toxicity in his system. As my brother left to go to work, I went to the phone to tell my mother the good news that, despite appearances, he seemed to be rallying, doing better.

One of the main difficulties of this two-and-a-half week journey was that it was so up and down: he was dying, no — he was o.k. and would live; I better stay because "this is it"; there is no way of telling when it will happen. This ambiguity was never more evident than when I returned to his room after my phone call.

Patrick J. Brennan

The drapery was pulled tightly around his bed. The emergency team stood around the bed. One nurse stood poised with what I surmise was an adrenalin shot, to directly shoot him in the heart.

"Father, we're losing him," a doctor said. "What do you want us to do, resucitate him? Should we give him the injection?" I looked at the team, helplessly. I looked to a friend who had just stopped in to visit. "I don't know what to do," I replied, shell-shocked and again surprised at this turn of events. A nurse spoke up. "Father Brennan, I'd let him go. If we 'shoot him' now, we'll have to 'shoot' him again in two hours and again tonight. Let him go!"

I said "Let him go." Then I approached his head and hands and held him. I cried, contained myself, then did what I have done for so many of my aging relatives. I told him to go home to his father, his mother, his brother, his sister and brother-in-law, his grandson. I kissed him and told him what a good "Pa" he had been. He blew a few more puffs of air, and . . . stopped.

"Is he gone?" I asked a nurse.

"Yes, he's gone."

I knelt down next to his bed and prayed. Learning trust and surrender prayer had been the initial conversion experience for me in my twenties. I never experienced the phenomenon of trust and surrender more profoundly than when I spiritually handed over, or surrendered my father.

PASCHAL JOURNEY

After his death, I drove home to tell my mother. Her primal screams could be heard throughout the condominium complex where we had recently helped them move. Upon notification, family members and friends began to gather to be with her, so that my brother and I could go to the funeral home — the same one that helped us bury my brother's neonate son 7 years before.

The Funeral

I spent the weekend preparing his wake and funeral. I decided somehow he ought to speak out to people in attendance; so with assistance, I cut out and reprinted "the best of" close to 40 pages of writing he had done in his final weeks. Because of the respirator he was on for the bulk of his time in the hospital, writing had become his basic mode of communicating. His scribblings and notes were scattered throughout his funeral booklet. I never thought that I would be able to preach at the funeral of either my mother or my father. Yet, when it was asked of me whether I was able, I was almost defiant: "Who else would do it." For the celebration and the preaching, I felt a new power, a higher power helping me. The funeral was a simple, beautiful celebration of him, a simple, uncomplicated, dedicated man. The post-communion hymn was (sorry, liturgists) *Tura Lura Lura,* and the recessional, a staccato rendition of *Amazing Grace* on bagpipes.

165

Patrick J. Brennan

The Aftermath

Deaths in the family necessitate role and rule reversals in terms of primary relationships. During this first anniversary marking of my father's death, I am doing a lot of remembering and a lot of recollecting on how his death changed my life. A good friend of mine, Bishop John Gorman, auxiliary bishop of Chicago, told me some time ago that the death of a parent, whenever it strikes — in adulthood or earlier — literally shakes the existential ground underneath your feet. That certainly had been true for me. I have added to my roles of archdiocese agency director, parish priest, national pastoral consultant, psychotherapist, the additional roles of condominium maintenance person and primary caretaker of my mother. It has been a brutal year, with much stress and time management confusion, as one role often has collided with another.

One dysfunctional thing that I have found myself doing is trying to become all things for my mother, especially to eradicate her grief and mine. I have gone through periods of omnipresence, to the point of canceling other important relationships. I have come to label this behavior as neither heroic nor virtuous, but toxic and co-dependent. Having grown up in an addictive environment, and having lost a loved one, despite all attempts at control, I have been in the posture the past year of trying to control, that is, stop another death — my mother's.

PASCHAL JOURNEY

On a winter night not too long ago, as I was nursing her through a bout with her own congestive heart failure syndrome, I was filled with both anxiety and anger at the prospect of losing another parent within one year. But, in a moment of rage and frustration, I angrily said words that are profoundly juxtaposed to my basic controlling posture toward life.

"If it's her time, God, take her."

Though the words were said in rage, even as I said them a great peace and serenity came over me. In different words, I was re-iterating the spirit of my initial conversion, when I suffered from extreme anxiety in my twenties. I was, and am, placing one of my most treasured people totally in the hands of a loving Creator-Parent, even if that meant or means the inevitable facing of physical death. That anger, surrender, peace experience has lead me over recent weeks and months to try to practice less an attitude of caretaking and control relative to my mother, and one of greater respect for what remains of her own adulthood and wanting to be her own person, and also to practice a surrender of her total being to the providential love of the Creator-Parent-God.

They say mid-life involves an awareness of limits. What I have seen in my role, in the death of my father and the care of my mother after his death, is a real attempt and need, on my part, to be God, to have no limits. As a spiritual director told me recently, "You have been trying to take better, more precise care of

Patrick J. Brennan

your parents than God does of the universe. At least in terms of compulsive detail, God doesn't control his universe as much as you try to control, especially, your mother." His words were like ice-water thrown in my face. I was trying to be God, greater than God. I often still fall into the same pattern.

I was struck recently by the wisdom of Dr. Bernard Shulman and Raeann Berman in their helpful and useful book, *How to Survive Your Aging Parents — So They and You Can Enjoy Life.* In their book, Shulman and Berman contend that often the behavior of a senior resembles that of a child, in its motivation and attempt to achieve a goal. Aging people, like children, often engage in behavior to: a) gain special attention, love, or service; b) exercise power, to hold onto status; c) hurt or take revenge on someone because they themselves are hurting; or d) a combination of any or all of these three.

Key to the mid-life child's health is understanding the aging parent's goal, which often is mis-directed, and not responding in kind, or engaging in the kind of response that perpetuates the game. Please take note: as a mid-life child I cannot change my parent or her misguided goal. I can only change my response which can either foster or eventually mitigate the manipulative behavior on the part of the parent.

Part of accepting mid-life limits is admitting and accepting one's status as "not God." Part of mid-life limits is also recognizing that seniors like children can become a never-ending well of needs and demands.

168

PASCHAL JOURNEY

In no way can a mid-life child provide for all of those needs and demands. What is needed is for the mid-life child to generate a network of caregivers who can support him/her in the effort of caring for a senior. What is needed is to allow a senior to do for the self as much as he or she possibly can. What is needed is for a mid-lifer to admit limits in the relationship, without guilt or compulsion. Without such an approach, the senior becomes someone clearly declining, but also with a hand and arm around the mid-life son or daughter, pulling them into a grave with them. The only question is who will physically die first?

August 25, 1990

So what was it like, the first anniversary of a family member's death. Anti-climatic! The wishing it would come and pass, the anticipation, the fear of how it would be, were all worse than the actual day. I dreamt about him, his grave, in fact, thought I heard his voice in the days preceding and following the first anniversary of his death — all signs of "anniversary reaction" they say, all signs that maybe at last I am beginning to bury my father.

. . . Through Faith

As I look back on the awful turbulence of these moments since my father's death, and the tremendous role and responsibility change it has thrust upon me, as well as the pain of his physical absence, I have often wondered, how have I, we as a family — he as patient

169

Patrick J. Brennan

— how did we get through this? I was reflecting on this recently when I came across a passage in scripture, the one involving Peter's profession of faith in Jesus as the Christ, the Promised One in *Matthew 16.*

After Peter proclaims conviction that Jesus is the Christ, Jesus says "Blessed are you Simon . . . flesh and blood has not revealed this to you, but my Father who is in Heaven." In indirect language, Jesus is equivalently saying "Good for you, Peter, if you have achieved a plateau of faith recognition; but please realize faith is a gift, perhaps mediated or given through human experience; but its real source (the real giver) is God."

As they say in African-American spirituality, if there has been any coping, survival, getting through, for me this past year, "We've gotten this far by faith." Faith is nothing I have earned or deserve. It has been transmitted to me as a gift.

You and I have gotten through, in fact, grown, through our personal losses and crises through the gift of faith.

- **Faith:** it is a personal relationship with a life-giving, spiritual presence.
- **Faith:** it is a helpful, positive vision of life.
- **Faith:** it is a way of behaving or living.
- **Faith:** it is a conviction that — no matter the degree of struggle or pain, God works learning, wisdom, growth, new and better life from all struggles.

170

PASCHAL JOURNEY

- **Faith:** sometimes it is not so much what we do, but awakening to what God is doing in our lives.

Faith is a gift — and each of us have gotten this far by faith.

Unfreezing Death

Organizational consultants speak of the need of some organizations to "unfreeze" certain non-life giving or producing practices. Several people over the course of the last months have pointed out to me how I seem frozen in death imagery. The years that I have invested in care-taking through multiple illnesses, almost deaths, actual deaths have, in a way, left me shell-shocked. In this aging family that I am a part of, my basic posture is and has been to wait for the next catastrophe, the next death.

I have begun to see how unhealthy and defensive such a posture is. At least one of my eyes has been focused on death in recent months, a real paralysis centering on hospitals, cemeteries, and impending loss. Call it Irish morbidity, or simply a natural defense mechanism, it is nonetheless, certainly not gospel living. I need to unfreeze this death pre-occupation with the Good News, that through the victory of the Resurrection, God has proven himself to be stronger than the forces of sickness, sin, death, and evil. The true disciples and apostles of Jesus Christ are witnesses to the empty tomb, not just the cross. I am convinced now that to allow one's self to be frozen in death imagery is to begin to get sucked into the forces of self destruction. The Good news is that death, in all of its forms, gives way to new life.

Choose Life!!!

For years, I had a button produced by the Pro-Life movement, which I attached to a lamp shade in the office where I did counseling. Though the movement obviously was attacking pro-abortion advocates, I used the button, for years, in a broadened sense to turn away from self-destructive, death-dealing values and relationships to more life-giving, truly fulfilling approaches to self, others, and life. I am dusting off that many-year-old button now, to remind myself that I have dwelled in the valleys of grief, fear, and apprehension long enough. I have been death-preoccupied too long. I want to live anew!

Spiritual Presence

One of the paradoxes of my life is that my father is more *really present* to me in death than he was in life. I often felt mistrust, estranged, alienated from him while we both were in the flesh. As he has moved to the realm of spirit, I have begun to experience a new kind of oneness with him. I speak to and pray through him daily. His death has been a re-affirmation of the Communion of Saints. I believe that I am more one with him now in the Holy Spirit. It is quite like, as James Loder writes in the *Transforming Moment*, the Emmaus journey. In that journey, for two disciples of

172

PASCHAL JOURNEY

Christ, an "unrecognized physical presence became a recognized, invisible, spiritual presence."

So it is with "Pa" and all of our loved ones.

I had surgery recently, an operation that my father said, before his death, he would help me with and at which he would be present. As I was wheeled into the operating room I knew he was there with me, though it was after his funeral.

Journal Questions for Individuals and Small Groups

1) Who is or was the most powerful loss in your life? Write or think about it.

2) Are you locked into images of death or life? In what ways? How would you like to change?

3) What are practical down-to-earth ways ordinary people, in everyday life can choose life?

4) Surface stories of physical absence that have become powerful spiritual presences.

Chapter Fourteen

Addiction: Lightning Strikes Close to Home

Bob

BOB, Robert, Doctor; it was always hard to get a handle on what to call this man, 8 years my senior, a mentor, a psychology professor, someone who would not counsel me in a period of crisis but referred me to someone less personally involved, more objective. It seemed that he longed for "Bob — like" friendships, but preferred "Robert-like" distancing, and was most comfortable in "Doctor," Ph.D formality. He entered my life at a very formative period — the end of undergraduate and the beginning of graduate school. He made me see the value of, indeed hunger for, the wisdom of the behavioral sciences, namely psychology. He helped me, if not in therapy, then in friendship gatherings to see the parallels between the insight, behavior change, and resistance process of psychotherapy, and the quite similar process of conversion or spiritual transformation. He also modeled for me what it meant to be an adult male in the world. In fact, he nudged me from being "southside shanty Irish," to knowing how to order in a nice restaurant, make hotel or flight reservations. He was one of my first significant mentors.

174

PASCHAL JOURNEY

I'm in my early forties now — about the time period he was in when trouble developed in our relationship. At the time, I was in the twenties to thirties transition. I began, in a sense, to have a life of my own, to develop both a persona and a reputation of my own existential authority. As most people do with most mentors, I had to break some ties to become my own person. Bob seemed to both like and dislike this process. He recognized it as healthy, but privately seemed to resent any of us who were becoming not even equal, but semi-peer to him in the helping professions. About eight years ago, over a dinner that I typically had to cancel because I double-scheduled, he (I would say) over-reacted and suggested that the whole relationship was in question. I, in turn, over-reacted by saying that if that was the way he wanted things, I was not about to fight or resist him. Though we have had minimal social contact in subsequent years, it was never the same. I had outgrown, and he had outgrown, our mentor-disciple relationship. Neither of us, counselors though we were in our own ways, seemed to know how to throw it, the relationship, into a different, better, new gear.

Rumors

In the last few years, rumors abounded about Bob — how he was losing jobs and positions. Some attributed it to neurological disorders, others to some form of substance abuse. I felt removed enough that I did not have to care. I do not feel proud of that posture;

175

but this is how I felt. He did not attend my father's wake or funeral. People said that he could not. But that significant absence at such a significant moment deepened the alienation.

A few weeks ago, rumors hit my desk that Bob was terminally ill. I was due to leave town with my family on a vacation, and I did not change my plans. In fact, a "go-between" friend said things were not as bad as rumors had suggested.

So, I went away, but, with a heavy heart, finding it hard to believe that someone who was gateway to my adulthood was having such a hard time finding his own way into and through his middle years. I resolved that upon my return, I would write him a letter, reminding him of the many of us whom he had helped — and how he could help himself if he mustered up enough energy and will power to re-direct himself. Of course, I would mention the co-operative role our wills play with God's grace.

No need for the homily. On my vacation, a call came in late afternoon. Bob had died. Apparently of liver malfunctioning.

I went and sat on a grassy hill in Wisconsin, where I was staying, the sun setting behind a hilly, rustic scene. I cried from the depths of my soul — for him: what the hell happened to him? For me: I lost a friend without reconciliation. For us: how much did he — if stories were and are current — simply mirror the self-destructive paths that many of us are on?

PASCHAL JOURNEY

A . . . holisms

In Greek, the letter *a* or the *alpha*, appearing as a prefix before a word is known as the *"privative alpha."* Privative refers to how the alpha functions to *deprive* the rest of the word of something. If "holos," in some way has to do with being *whole, a-holism* must refer to anything that makes us non-whole, or rob us of integrity. That can be, as we discussed in another section — a substance like alcohol or drugs, a person or a relationship, or even an organization.

Most of the rumors converged that Bob was in an a-holism, an addiction. Again, addictions end only in awakening, intervention and recovery; or death. Bob resisted all efforts from people, much closer to him than I, to confront and begin to co-operate with God in transforming his addiction.

He died. "What a waste! What a tragedy!" sympathizers said at the wake, as they viewed his jaundiced, battered body. How terrifying, I thought — he apparently chose this.

Deadly Addiction

Several of us gathered after Bob's death to reflect on his loss. I probably am the most "highly credentialed," and resourced of the lot, at least in terms of psychology. I was wailing on that I could not believe that this happened to Bob — mentor, model to us all. I could not believe he died because of substance abuse.

Patrick J. Brennan

A much more humble and common sense man then said, "You simply do not know the power of addictions do you? There is a turning point in the process — a point of no return. They kill you." I was reminded, again, the maxim: a person either gets *consumed by a process* of addiction *or* begins to *work a process* of life-giving, therapeutic attitudes and behaviors.

From the Dark Mirror

Bob's coffin has been a kind of darkened mirror in which many of us see reflections of ourselves. Our disbelief is really a denial that deadly lightning can strike so close to home, so close to us. What do I mean by a dark-mirror reflection? So many of us are in a process of some sort of self-destruction — by the way we eat, drink, smoke, worry, work, generate stress. Many of us are on a parallel road to Bob's. The Church and other organizations that refuse to admit that their need for help, healing, and recovery are also on a self-destructive road. Many of us see ourselves, as individuals and as a Church, in Bob; and we are frightened. Bob's death spoke to our impending mid-life mortality. He was only eight years older than I, and he literally committed suicide, slowly, progressively, gradually through alcoholism. As only God can do, he spoke through a tragedy, the self-induced death of a relatively young man, God asked: In what ways are you self-destructive? Do you want to continue on this collision course with death? You have options: you are neither a victim nor a martyr.

178

PASCHAL JOURNEY

Anger at Non-Integrity

I guess I felt another level of anger toward Bob. It is probably an anger I have toward myself too and also toward many of us in ministry or the helping professions. The anger is toward a lack of integrity. More than anyone I knew, Bob wore the persona of perfection, apparently totally dedicated to wholistic living, *wellness* as it is sometimes called. Apparently, as I write this in anger after the early stages of recovery from his death, he talked wellness; he talked wholistic health. But hidden beneath the wrappings of his life he was rotting himself out. I have heard that friends closer to him than I, had intervened in recent years, offering to him totally financed recovery programs, all done in anonymity. He refused treatment. He could not exercise the vulnerability needed to accept help.

In my anger, I again saw a reflection, and I became frightened. To what degree do I not live what I preach and teach? How many people did Bob hurt, let down by revealing he did not practice or live what he preached? How many people will I de-power, people whom I mentor, if I do not consciously practice the spirituality and therapeutic vision that I espouse? His death has made me feel terribly responsible for and to those to whom I minister and whom I counsel. What happens to fibrillating people when they discover the guru, in a sense, was or is cardboard, without existential rootedness in his/her articulated, life-giving vision. *Their* fear or despair can only deepen.

179

Patrick J. Brennan

Revelation

If there is any theological point to be made here, it is that God does not cause, but can use, the worst of situations to reveal, to manifest Himself, and to speak a unique message to each of us. Bob's death was a powerful message from God to me about the sacredness of life, the deceit of pretense, and the possibility for all of us of self-destruction. I share it with you to facilitate and expand God's revelation.

Euphemisms

After I told Bob's story at a gathering recently, a woman stood in line to speak to me. She approved of the general nature of my message. But she did have one critique. As I talked of Bob, I spoke of his "substance abuse." She wanted to know why I chose a euphemism rather than "alcoholism." I countered that the cause of his death was still under controversy, that his death could have been prescription drug related.

She wanted to know what I was afraid of, why I was afraid. Were we as an institution as Church, or Bob's primary relationship group, afraid to use the word "alcoholism." Were we cerebrally accepting, but emotionally in denial?

I think she was and is right. That someone could have died of alcoholism under my nose is unacceptable to me. That someone could have been so totally self-destructive without my knowing it is totally unacceptable to me. In my resistance to the apparent truth

180

is there denial? And is there denial because I have difficulty in accepting that we all have the potential to destroy ourselves; and that frightens me. The woman's suspicions are accurate. I am having difficulty in accepting the reflection that Bob is of so many of our lives.

I feel that I cannot, but I must. I will. And I will try to learn from the experience.

"What profit would someone show, if that person were to gain the whole world and destroy him or herself in the process. What can a person offer in exchange for the self?"

—Matthew 16:26

Journal Questions for Individuals
and Small Groups

1) Are there any ways that you are self-destructive? List all such patterns.

2) What of the above patterns need your immediate attention, or are screaming out for change?

3) What are the self-destructive patterns that we see in primary relationships or our own peer groups?

4) What are the self-destructive patterns in generations younger than we? How can we serve as a corrective?

Chapter Fifteen

Reconciliation: Beyond the Confessional

"If your brother should commit some fault against you, go and, point out his fault, but keep it between the two of you. . . . If he does not listen . . . summon another. . . . If he ignores them, refer it to the Church. If he ignores even the Church, then treat him as you would a Gentile or a tax collector. I assure you, whatever you declare bound on earth, shall be bound in heaven; and whatever you declare loosed on earth, shall be held loosed in heaven."

Mt. 18: 15-18

An Intervention

AN OLD friend of mine asked to see me recently. He was rather mercurial in his approach to setting up the appointment, preferring neither a restaurant, nor any public place, but rather an apartment he owns as an investment with someone else. Because I have a great respect for the man, I of course, willingly saw him. He began his comments that Friday morning with some affirmation, reminding me of my gifts and talents. Then, he switched gears. "I am about to say some things that may make you angry, may make you

182

leave, and not talk to me anymore. But what I am about to say, I say out of love and friendship."

I gulped in apprehension, but I so trust him, I said, "Go ahead!"

"Pat, you're addicted!"

"Addicted!" I responded. "To what?"

"To your mother, caretaking her and your family — and to work. Another friend knows I'm doing this, and she agrees with it. You've cut people out of your life. You're not available for time off. With you, it is just work and family, work and family. It is almost as if you don't have a life. I hear kids saying 'Get a life.' I guess I'm saying that to you. And I am saying all this so that you don't die a premature death, self-destruct."

He went on. "I want you to talk concretely about how you can change your behavior — to have more space, to be less stressed-out, to recreate a life for yourself. I'll call during the week to see what you're going to do. But I'll go beyond this to other people, and to your family and other friends, to get them to intervene. I've had other friends self-destruct. I won't stand by and watch you do it."

As I drove home, I was a bit angry at and humbled by what had transpired; but I knew he was right. Work and family responsibilities have been making life unmanageable. If that is an indicator of addiction or compulsion, then, I am afflicted with such a problem. Since that talk, to now as I write, I am seeking God's help in renewing my own spiritual program, re-prioritizing

Patrick J. Brennan

responsibilities in my life, that I may have greater peace of heart.

My friend did an intervention on me. Interventions are a rather new technique in treating compulsive disorders. As a technique, it flies in the face of old conventional wisdom. That wisdom basically said that people change or grow when they hurt enough; so, let them bottom out on alcohol, in an economic ruin, ruin their health, at least partially self-destruct. At that point of rock bottom, maybe someone will change.

Interventionists, on the other hand, say that it may be too late if we wait for someone's life going askew to intervene, to gently challenge. Notice what my friend did for me. He began with affirmation, then moved to challenge and the challenge was not a put down at all, but done with assertiveness, love, and respect.

I think that there might be more enduring relationships, healthier people, less compulsive self destructive behavior if more of us learned to gently confront, challenge, intervene, rather than ignoring dysfunctional behavior, engaging in avoidance behaviors, or sweeping obvious problems under the rug. I also think that indirectly Jesus was speaking about "intervention," in the eighteenth chapter of Matthew.

Reconciliation as Intervention and Process

What Jesus is addressing directly is reconciliation. As I have stated in other writings, our approach to reconciliation, at least in the Catholic Church, has become anemic and impoverished. "Going to confession" for years has bumped, replaced "existential reconciliation." Existential, real life reconciliation is both a) an intervention; and b) a process. If someone feels sinned against or hurt, or realizes he or she has hurt another or sinned against another, there can be the typical denial, avoidance, sweeping-under-the-rug patterns, or an intervention in which one or both parties take the initiative to begin catharsis, communication, and gentle confrontation with each other. Usually in situations of sin or hurt, one such encounter is not enough. If there is a sufficient amount of buried hurt, many such encounters, some involving a third party, or prayer, or ritual, or sacrament are needed.

In other words, confession of sin or hurt, admission of need for God's help and that of the community, all is a process that may gradually lead us to some sort of Church encounter or ritual. What we have done in fact is truncate "process," even in the renewal of the sacrament of reconciliation in the mid-seventies. Two of my other books, *Penance and Reconciliation: Guidelines for Contemporary Catholics* (Thomas More) and *The Reconciling Parish* (Tabor) document some of the history in the abbreviation and diminishing of the *intervention process* of reconciliation.

Let us keep in mind here also the father of the Church, Tertullian's original meaning of *sacramentum*, or sacrament. The original Latin word meant *to vow*. At the time, the rites of initiation, Baptism, Confirmation, and Eucharist, came to be known as sacraments, a process and ritual of *vowing*. As *reconciliation* of sinners and apostates emerged as a parallel process, it was clearly seen to be a way of *re-vowing* to a reality that a person somehow had strayed from, namely the Kingdom living originally vowed at initiation. In any attempt to re-vivify the sacrament of reconciliation, or reconciliation as an intervention and process, we must keep in mind what we are doing is attempting to help ourselves and others live more fully the meaning of Baptism.

Reconciliation: Healing Hurt

There are people incapable of intimacy because of rejection in the past, men who rape now who were physically or sexually abused as children, people emotionally crippled because of addictions in their home of origin, and on and on. In case after case in spiritual direction and counseling, I encounter folks having trouble in *the now* of their lives, because of *buried hurt* from the past of our lives. Thus, John Bradshaw, and others teach about the importance of returning, on the level of image and imagination to times in our lives when we either felt abandoned or abused, and look at, and dwell within it, and seek divine help in healing hurt — even though scar tissue will always remain. Bradshaw and others suggest that this often involves a returning to a damaged, hurt inner child. But it need not just be *the child* era that we return to. Some of us have equally acquired clusters of pain in *adulthood* that have become buried hurt. Buried deep within us, they are a time bomb still going off in us, still robbing us of joy, still keeping us from intimacy.

In passing on to us the mission and ministry of "binding and loosing," Jesus wants us to heal each other's wounds, really, existentially. And there is a promise in the admonition or mandate. There is no hurt that God's power and our honest facing of issues, and dialoguing with each other cannot heal.

Reconciliation: Freeing From Addiction, Compulsion, and Entrapment

As mentioned earlier, recent estimates are that over 90% of the American population is addicted, that is, have an over-attachment to someone or something, that, in effect, becomes life-robbing rather than life giving. In addictive processes there is a gradual build-up of need for or tolerance of a substance, a relation-ship, or way of doing things. Concommitantly, there is a perversion of integrity, and a loss of a sense of original vision or mission. In Western culture, we grow addicted to substances, dysfunctional relation-ships, systems or ways of doing things, and organi-zations.

There are several things that can happen to in-dividuals or corporate groups in the process of addiction:

1) *denial:* This is the hallmark of addiction, in both those directly influenced by the addiction and those addicted to the addictive person or process

Patrick J. Brennan

— the co-dependent. Denial, avoidance, sweeping under the rug, only make more toxic the already addictive waters. Primary addictions necessitate back-up or sub-addictions to sustain themselves. For example, the workaholic may also become an alcoholic and or a prescription drug abuser.

2) *breakdown:* Breakdown is an integrating, comprehensive term for acute pain, wherein one experiences the pain and experience of limits. Often in an addictive process be it to a substance, a relationship, an organization, or anything else that may be life-robbing, one reaches the point of the declaration of bankruptcy — emotionally, relationally, and spiritually. The breakdown can indeed be a blessing. If the person receives the right kind of support, mentoring, and aid in development of a spiritual program, he or she may actually experience John Bradshaw's steps of recovery. They are:

   - to *re-cover* the past and present, taking assessment of the distorted nature one's life has taken on;
   - to *uncover* a lost self, buried over by habit, compulsion, and addiction;
   - to finally begin to *discover* the true self God wills, has willed the person to be and become.

3) *death:* If the denial in the addictive process remains frozen, death is a necessary consequence. The death is actually a process, that involves the *gradual* death of many different aspects of a person's life — health, relationships, spirituality, and then, the eventual death of one's physical self.

Since the birthing of A.A. and The Twelve-Step process, it has been emphasized that the root cause of addictions (in addition to some genetic, physical factor in some cases) is a spirituality problem. The reconciliation offered a "trapped person" through the twelve-step process, sponsoring, and development of a spiritual program have proven to be the only long-lasting, effective process of recovery. Note again, one is always recovering, reconciling, and never done.

Reconciliation: God's Forgiveness of Sin

Many of us who grew up in the scrupulosity-prone church of by-gone years, often would go through periods of protracted guilt, never quite believing that God could actually forgive our sins. In actuality, we often had a distorted notion of both sin and God. A scriptual view of sin reveals that sin is at root attitudinal, subtly lurking in the mind and heart. It then expresses itself in behavior. Sin leads to sins. Sin may be personal, enfleshed in the self; or it may be corporate, and the individual may share in it, reflectively or non-reflectively.

Patrick J. Brennan

The Old Testament portrays God as one beckoning us to turn from sin, which is always an over-attachment to someone or something, or idolatry, and turn back to him. This turning is called *metanoia*. Jesus in the New Testament consistently portrays God as One who forgives sin. The parables and teachings of Jesus certainly say this. Perhaps equally important, Jesus's behavior sacramentalized or said, forgiveness is the nature of God. Thus, Luke's gospel especially teaches us that Jesus spent significant time with sinners and tax collectors. This significant time with the marginal and marginated was a statement that the Kingdom of God — God's power, love, and forgiveness — extend to all people.

The experience of reconciliation in the early Church, in the days after Christ's glorification, came to resemble the steps and stages of the catechumenate. Those in serious sin, who had rather clearly in their behavior said no to God and community engaged in a step-by-step process of prayer, penance, support by the community, gradual life change and return to the Table of the Lord, or Eucharist. For those in less serious sin, the ancient Jewish practices of prayers of contrition and works of penance, like fasting, were regularly engaged in.

The Old and New Testament, plus the early practices of the Church, reveal, then, a beautiful and rich tradition of people, indeed, wrestling with their own demons and those of the culture, but also responding, *really, existentially* to the invitation of God to come home to His forgiveness. I stress the words *really* and *existentially* because, as a friend, Fr. Bob Blondell, from the Archdiocese of Detroit, frequently says, too many Catholics have made reconciliation into an anemic ritual of "spin dry" confession. I greatly value the sacramental moment of the Rite of Penance, but I am suggesting that the life change and process that I just spoke of must be restored in Catholic consciousness if we are to experience forgiveness and *real-life* new beginnings in the fullest sense.

Forgiving Each Other

A final dimension of reconciliation I ask us to consider is the act of forgiving others. I spoke with a kind of "whiner" friend recently, who constantly hark-ins back to people and experiences that have hurt him. He is frozen in time; and has frozen people who have hurt him within his own spirit. After a recent barrage of complaints, I leveled a not-too-therapeutic comment at him — out of frustration. I said: "Do you think you're the only one who's been hurt in the world? I have been hurt. Everyone has been hurt. It's important to get beyond the hurt and not be paralyzed by it."

I do not want to pretend I do not at times get lost in my own resentments and grudges. But I also know that it is not healthy for me to stay in such a position. I need to do, when such times occur, some forgiveness/ reconciliation work. Thus when people ask me how

Patrick J. Brennan

can they forgive someone who has significantly hurt them, I can only answer from my own experience. When I am hurt, I try to:

1) enter into the hurt and name it; the opposite is to deny (ignore) it, sweep it under the rug, or obsess about it;
2) make a decision: I am going to forgive this person;
3) pray for the grace, or divine help to forgive; for forgiveness is not part of our animal instincts; to retaliate is;
4) act "as if," or practice responding to the given person as if I've forgiven him or her; frequently behavior change can spark emotional and attitudinal change;
5) engage in an assertive, non-put down honesty session, or sessions, with the people or person involved.

You do not need a doctorate to understand or practice the above five steps. But so many people fail to. They seem to prefer to clutch onto anger and resentment. The clutching keeps them from the unchartered waters of reconciliation and Kingdom living. Many of us fear where the Spirit of God is leading us; so holding on to anger is a great way to resist God.

Conclusion

I am glad that friend of mine cared enough to risk losing my friendship, to intervene on my self-destructive ways. He pushed me off shore to a journey of reconciliation and healing. And he helped me to understand reconciliation in more profound terms: as healing of hurt, liberation from addictive ways, being forgiven, and learning to forgive — none of which can be done without the greater intervention by a loving, healing God.

Journal Questions for Individuals and Small Groups

1) Is there anyone with whom you could make amends without causing greater hurt or problems? Name the person or people. Pray for God's grace to act on your insights.

2) Make lists, prayerfully, of areas where you need reconciliation: hurt, addictive habits, sin, having been sinned against. Commit the four areas to prayer.

3) Share or reflect on a story from your life that speaks of a need for healing and reconciliation.

4) Alone or in a group, name your favorite story from Scripture about healing or reconciliation. Share or reflect on why this particular story speaks to your heart.

Chapter Sixteen

What Have We Done to the Good News?

SO OFTEN my work leads me to spend a lot of time doing analysis of systems and organizations — how are our church delivery systems working? I do not think I spend enough time reflecting on the actual "product" we offer to the world, the good news. As a director of religious education asked me recently, "What's good about the good news?" She was asking me to think about that to try to present some *bare bones* proclamation of the gospel to a group of parents. Paul VI put it another way in his rhetorical question in *Evangelii Nuntiandi* (1975). "Has the Good News lost its power . . . to change lives, to transform society?"

I do not think the good news has lost any of its power to change lives. I do think, however, the Good News has been muted by two forces: the voice of consumer America, which uses the bully pulpit of the media, to evangelize pagan values; and a church that is at best, out-moded in its strategies, or perhaps more to the point — a horse and buggy still struggling along in a jet-age world. I will speak more about these two phenomena later.

194

PASCHAL JOURNEY

The Good News: Vision

Two stories struck me recently, stories about two young men of about the same age living in the same town. One has spina bifida. At age 22, he has lived much longer than anyone has expected him to. Though he can move nothing from his shoulders down, his outlook is almost always positive, hopeful, and optimistic. His mother says that a great deal of the vision he has comes from a closeness that he feels with God. He is truly convinced that God loves him despite the circumstances of his life. His faith and outlook are so powerful that he inspired a neighbor to return to active Church participation after years of being away.

This man has a classmate, who unlike him "has everything." God blessed him with health, looks, athletic ability, intelligence. Several weeks ago, mysteriously, he took his own life. No one knows why. He "exited" without explanation.

I do not wish to moralize over or about a suicide. A lot could have been going on in the latter young man's life that pushed him to the point of self-destruction. But at least the suicide throws into relief, or highlights the power that faith brings to the life of the first young man.

The young man who wants to live despite his spina bifida has achieved at least part of what the good news is, an outlook, or a vision of life, flowing from his relationship with God and community. Paradoxically, core to this "good news vision" is a conviction about "the life, death, and resurrection nature" of living. We call this the "paschal mystery." Paschal simply means *passage.* Christ has passed from death to life. And so shall we. There is great *promise* in this vision. For not only Christ, but all of us also live lives that are "passage" in nature. Each day the little disappointments and also the major difficulties associated with human becoming are little deaths, which, if approached in faith, always give way to new life, growth, wisdom, and becoming. The whole process goes on over and over in our lives until the final passage. Christ has conquered evil, death, sin, and suffering. Through faith, we can share in the victory.

We use theological language to describe the foundation of this good news vision. We speak of "redemption," "salvation," "liberation." What is important to keep in mind is that we participate in redemption, salvation, and liberation in actuality *now.* But its fulfillment awaits us in the future. This is truly good news!

The Good News: The Communion of Saints

The good news is life-changing stuff; if only we did not make it old, boring, institutionalized news. A natural development of the paradoxically positive paschal vision that I just spoke of is a core conviction that even when we lose those who are most precious to us in death, they live on in spirit, and we can have a new, unique relationship with them. As I mentioned earlier, my father is a physical absence to me now, because he has physically died. But he is an ever more real emotional, spiritual presence to me. Maybe I am just an old-fashioned Irishman who learned his Baltimore Cathechism too well, but I firmly believe in the Communion of Saints.

Thus, the many people who have physically passed out of my life through death live on in my heart, and in another dimension of life that I could not even try to explain — eternal life: father, aunts, uncles, nephew, best friend. And I speak to them daily, asking that they intercede for me and the people I love. As I ask us to reflect on the difference the good news makes in our lives, the most significant one for me, during these middle years of loss, is the promise of eternal life. Without the promise and my conviction about eternal life, life would have much less meaning for me.

The Good News: The Power of Prayer

Let us explain further what is life-changing, or good about the good news. A first grade religion teacher told me recently that she is trying to emphasize the importance of informal conversation with God, over the rote memorization and recitation of prayers. Thus, she encourages her children to speak directly to God from their hearts. In so advising, she is introducing children to someone psychiatrist Daniel Elkind suggests the mainline churches are failing to pass on to children: *the companion God*. A companioning God is ever-

Patrick J. Brennan

present, ever-available, and open to the sharing of all feelings and thoughts. Boston-based journalist Donald Feder wrote recently that the development of a prayer and spiritual life could be as advantageous as counseling and psychotherapy in stemming the self-destructive tendencies of many young people. Robert Bellah called us in *Habits of the Heart* to become communities of memory — more reflective people. Allan Bloom did the same thing in *The Closing of the American Mind.* God is as close as our prayer. That is truly good news! We never walk alone. That is more than the title of a song. It is a core conviction that leads to a life of praying.

The Good News: Grace

The good news about prayer necessitates a comment about the felt experience flowing from prayer — *grace.* Grace, divine presence freely given to us, is that power greater than ourselves that we can attend to, tap into which provides us with help, and, comfort, and challenge. Medieval theology nuanced, rather academically, the many different types of grace. I personally never found metaphysical approaches to faith too helpful. What is helpful to me is experiential, existential theology and spirituality. I can *feel,* have *felt grace,* probably — at times when I have deliberately prayed, and other times as free gift — or uninvited presence. Sometimes that presence — invited or uninvited — has been comforting. At other times that presence has been

198

disturbing, challenging me to more profound conversion and transformation of life.

The Good News: The Trinity

Our God is loving Parent. That is good news! Our God is lover, norm for living, rabbi, teacher, redeemer — the one who brings us back to where we are meant to be — that is good news! Our God is Spirit, grace, spiritual presence — comforting and challenging. That is good news! The doctrine of the Trinity is a symbolic way of saying that our God is more than one living as one. We further unravel the good news: we are made in God's image. As God is *communion* — more than one as one, so we are called to mirror God — in family, friendships, small groups, parish, Church universal: we are more than one striving to live as one. This is what we mean by the Catholicity of our Church — not uniformity, but a quest for living in communion amidst diversity.

Leonardo Boff tries to break open the beauty of "the Trinity as reflection of us" and "us as reflection of the Trinity" in his book *Trinity and Society,* wherein he uses phraseology like "from the solitude of one to the communion of three," and "in the beginning there was communion."

Boff as theologian is saying what Stephen Covey as management consultant and behavioral scientist says in the *Seven Habits of Highly Effective People.* Covey says Americans and many in Western society

Patrick J. Brennan

have been trained to define maturity as independence. Covey speaks of *Synergy,* the discovery that *alone* is never *as* joyful or effective an experience as *together.* The Trinitarian: nature of the good news, the call to communion in imitation of God, flies in the face of the loneliness and individualism of our age and culture.

The Good News: Reconciliation

We believe that there is no hurt, emotional or spiritual, past or present, that cannot be healed by the higher power, God. We believe that there is no addiction or compulsion from which we cannot be liberated by the power of God. We believe that there is no sin which God will not forgive. We believe that there is no one who has hurt us whom we cannot forgive by the power of God. This four told mystery we call reconciliation. It is truly good news in a world of brokeness, addiction, resentment, and power.

The Good News: Sacraments

Evolving from the Church's ancient rites of initiation, there have evolved seven sacred rituals that we call *sacraments.* Again, the original meaning of *sacramentum* is, "the taking of a vow." Every time someone celebrates a sacrament, they are in effect *vowing* to the person and meaning system of Jesus and to His living body today, the Church. Adrian van Kaam and Susan Muto, in *Commitment: Key to Christian*

Maturity maintain that it is living a committed life that is one of the chief hallmarks of a fulfilled, mature life. In a culture advocating, as John Kavanaugh writes in *Following Christ in a Consumer Society,* not being too committed to anything or anyone, our sacramental life is a counter-culture celebration of the committed life. As I alluded to before, however, sacraments have been trivialized, have become cultural milestones, robbed of evangelical power — certainly not the powerful celebrations of conversion and vowing that they could be.

The Good News: Morality

Many years ago, John Glaser, a moral theologian, told a group of us that morality is essentially responsibility for the gift of life. As an ecclesial body, we stand for something — responsibility for creation, for life, and specifically human life in all of its forms. We are *gifted* people; and we remind the world of the need to *respond well* (responsibly) to and for the gift. This view lifts morality out of the realm of should's and ought's and moral discernment out of the realm of scrutinizing whether we have been "good boys and girls." We are guardians of morality, that is responsible living. This is truly good news.

The Good News: Politicization

When Americans hear the word "politics" their minds jump to *Democratic* or *Republican.* But the notion of politics has a broader meaning. Politicization refers to the taking of action. In the context of faith, it refers to putting our faith into action. There are often unnecessary walls placed between Church, world, and Kingdom of God. Leonardo Boff and many liberation theologians have written eloquently about this. If the Kingdom is going to be enfleshed anywhere, it is *in the world*. We need not inherit society as it is being given to us; we are not victims and martyrs. We can re-shape the whole tone of society, ushering in the New Age, a new Creation; God's reign. Unfortunately, both in terms of spirituality and political conformity, Americans seem content to sit back and allow specialists, like clergy and politicians, to shape life for them. We have lost much of the sense of personal responsibility that characterized the early Christian movement and the vision of the American founding fathers and mothers. Evangelization, wrote Paul VI in *Evangelii Nuntiandi,* is the transformation of society with the power of the gospel. That we can do that is good news.

Good News: Off of the Ladder of Success

One of western society's images or metaphors for success is to be on the ladder of success. So many people have, figuratively, climbed the ladder and found little of lasting worth at the top. Those who have experienced conversion, or spiritual transformation have experienced something almost diametrically opposed to the ladder of success. It is a spiraling downward into the mystery of life, love, and being. The human experiences that lead a person into those spiral types of experience have led to much more meaning and joy then "ladder experiences."

Conclusion:
Unleashing the Good News

The core good news of Scripture, the good news of our tradition is truly life-changing stuff — if only we would unleash its power. Faith, the good news, can only be conveyed by culture. As I said at the outset, the dominant culture of consumerism is currently speaking "in a louder voice," muting the power of the good news. Similarly outmoded ecclesiology, or theology of Church, and strategies for doing parish or Church render the good news "old," "bad," or "institutional."

There is need for parishes and institutions to renew an educational ecology, or a culture of faith, in which parish and family (in its many adapted forms) work together in imparting to people of all ages the great difference good news, gospel living involves. Unless we do, we will increasingly be a Church of baptized pagans.

Journal Questions for Individuals and Small Groups

1) Is there an element of the good news being muted in your life? How could you reclaim its power?

2) Key to gospel living is joy. Are you joyful? What brings you joy, or diminishes your joy?

Patrick J. Brennan

3) Does liturgy at your parish communicate good news? How or how not? How many of you would be willing to share your evaluations with your pastor?

4) In what areas of your or each other's lives is there a need now for God's grace and prayer?

Chapter Seventeen

Holy Communion: Coming Home Again

A COUPLE of weeks ago, I baptized my newly born niece, Katie. Because of the children present, I tried to express the magic of the moment by telling stories.

"Once upon a time," I said, "we waited, as a family for a very long time for a baby to be born into our family. Then, we were blessed with a little girl. Her name is Heather." I looked at my niece, eight years old. She was assisting me at the Baptism. She smiled glowingly.

"Once upon a time we waited for another baby. And he came, Justin, Heather's brother. But Justin was a very sick baby; he stayed with us only a day. And then he died, or went home to God. The pain of his leaving convinced us of how precious each child is." I looked at Heather. Big tears rolled down her cheeks — the first time in seven years I saw her communicate any emotion about the brother that she never knew, the brother who died when she was only about a year old. I continued: "But God works good even out of apparently bad things: now we have a saint in heaven who intercedes for us in prayer, with Jesus, and he is still with us in the Holy Spirit." I put my arm around Heather as I continued; I was trying also to contain my own repressed emotions.

Patrick J. Brennan

"And once upon a time, God blessed us with another gift, Katie, who I am sure will grow to be a precious, beautiful girl, like Heather." I truncated the rest of my words, trying to convey to my family in abbreviated fashion, because of the high emotion, some deeply held convictions I hold after my years of both celibacy and family counseling. Among the convictions are: the great gift of children, the best gift *to* children is working at a good marriage, and how the most real experience of Church is prayer, love, reconciliation, and graced meals at home, in the domestic church.

After the ceremony I expressed surprise to my brother and his wife at Heather's reaction to my mentioning of her brother. They were not surprised. Kathy, my sister-in-law, told me Justin is a very large image in Heather's consciousness. My brother concurred. After we were alone, I asked Heather if her tears indicated that I had made her sad. She told me she was not sad at all.

No — it was not sadness. Though she does not have the words to convey it, Justin, though never seen or met, is very much a part of Heather's *home.*

Sometime around the time of Katie's Baptism, I mustered up enough courage to do something. My father passed away about a year and a half ago. About six months before his death, faced with the inevitability of his terminal illness, both he and my mother asked me to facilitate the sale of our family home, a house on the south side of Chicago. We had been there since I was 3½ years old, that is, 38 years. To make

206

PASCHAL JOURNEY

a long, agonizing story short, my brother and I arranged the sale of the house and the passover of my parents to the Promised Land of a suburban condo. A difficulty that I had for over a year after the sale was that I could not go back and look at *home*. Friends kiddingly challenged me to go back and look. I, in fact, was close to the house for various reasons, many times. But it was like a reverse magnetic force — I was propelled away from my house/home. I could not face the vulnerable pain of going back to look at a home I did not want to leave, but was, in effect, "thrown out of" by history and circumstances.

I could not go back . . . until, one day recently, I explained my feelings about all this in a talk. A woman came up to me and said: "Go, go look at it again; celebrate the memories of home, and be glad that the bricks, wood, cement, and glass are becoming a happy home to other people." I filed her challenge far back in the "to be gotten to" file, until recently, when I felt both the need and the courage to go back and face home.

That morning, as I got closer to the street that I had deliberately avoided for over a year, my heart began to pound rapidly. I was feeling the beginning of a panic attack. I turned off the radio. I wanted quiet, as I experienced this strange phenomenon. As I got closer to the house, the words to an old African-American revival song came to mind. "This is holy ground . . . this is holy ground. . . ." I hummed to myself. Finally, I made the turn onto the block of 79th and Fairfield,

and for the first time in 15 months, stared at . . . home.
. . . My heart stopped pounding. I felt like I had x-ray
vision. I could tell people about every nuance and
crevice in that structure. As I looked I felt how much
I loved that house . . . I love that house. I drove around,
parked in the alley and looked at the backyard and the
back of the house. I drove around and parked in front,
and stared. I felt a strange peace. I always loved that
house. But finally I realized that it was no longer home
for me. It is a house that I will always love. But it is
no longer home. "Home" is the people and experiences that I encountered there, who are now in my
memory, some of whom have died but with whom I
am one in spirit. "Home" is the people and experiences that are currently part of my life — even the
apparent "exile" in a suburban condo. I moved, in that
experience, from exile to home.

I recently celebrated a multi-racial, multi-ethnic
liturgy as the close of a day-long conference. A powerfully gifted African-American female soloist sang a
song as part of the Liturgy of the Word. As she sang
I saw one woman, a black woman, "get the Spirit."
She was so powerfully moved by the song she fell to
the floor and began to scream "My Lord, My Lord."
Having worked at African-American revivals before
I was aware that such occurrences are rather common
at such gatherings. I was apprehensive, however,
about the reactions to the incident from the rest of the
congregation, which was largely white. Specifically,
I was most concerned about my mother's reaction. She

was in the congregation, and is not one to appreciate effusive expressions of emotion at worship. For her, church services should be short, to the point, respectful, and not too sociable in nature.

Thus, after the ceremony, I was waiting to take my punishment like a man; but I was surprised at my mother's reaction.

"Pat," she said, "when that woman sang, and that other woman got so emotional, I began to cry. I cried through the whole mass.

"Why did you cry?" I asked.

"For the first time since he died I felt your father's presence and could see him in his gray suit. It's the first time it happened to me since his death."

For several days after the service, she spoke of recurring episodes of seeing him and sensing him. I tried to explain to her that I have felt his presence a lot since his death. That experience, I believe, is a gift, a gift of divine consolation. After fifteen months of grief, bitterness, and her own physical decline, robbed of her house and husband, my mother has finally begun to feel at home again.

Home . . . it is not a place. It is rather a state of mind. It is what Erik Erikson called years ago "identity," a general feeling of well-being about ourselves, feeling at ease in our own skin. 2) Home is not a place; it is intimacy especially with people we call "primary relationships." 3) Home is not a place, rather it is a communion that exists between ourselves and those who have gone before us in death. 4) Home: it is not a place, but the communion that exists between ourselves and God who loves us unconditionally, is ever present to us as Spirit, and who works all things to our good, even life's painful moments.

Home, it is such a simple reality, but it is also so elusive for so many of us. It has become elusive because of the values of the "counter-gospel" around us, values like independence, isolation, fragmentation in and loss of relationships and intimacy, the massive de-valuing of the relational and the personal, expanding materialism and consumerism, the loss of vulnerability and willingness to be wounded that is needed for love and commitment. To sum up, there has been in our culture a devaluing of relational matters. There has been also a devaluing of the interior life. Jesuit teacher William O'Malley said recently, "We've forgotten that essentially we are souls, spirits." Thus, we have become a people with a lot of houses, places, things, but without homes.

Part of being at home in the world is having an ease about the self, identity, a healthy ego strength. Madonna Kolbenschlag, in her book, *Lost in the Land of Oz* writes about the wounded consciousness of our culture that has rendered many of us orphan-like in our approach to life. We orphans have a lust for material things, inflated expectations regarding success and productivity, but dashed hopes, low-grade anxiety, and depression. As orphans, people of our age and culture have feelings of abandonment, deprivation, loneliness, mourning, and a lack of nurturance in our relationships. These relational experiences have contributed to the development of misguided notions about ourselves, flawed visions and mis-informed outlooks on life. Many of us stand in need of massive re-education of our self concept. We are not what we have. We are not what we do. We need to discover the true self. Kolbenschlag suggests that many of us are like Dorothy in the Wizard of Oz, ripped from rootedness and identity; the tornado in our case is our culture. She admonishes her reading and lecture audiences: stop surrendering so gently to Oz, get critical about societal values and what they are contributing to the malformation of the self. We need to get back to Kansas, home, the true self that God willed in the womb.

Part of being at home in the world is the discovery of intimacy — in and out of marriage. One ex-priest told me recently that in the seminary he was trained not to have special relationships with men. Neither was he to be close with women. "Wasn't I prepared well," he mused, "to work with people?" Maybe that man's seminary training is a glimpse of many people's experiences of growth and relationships. Most of us received little or no training in human relations skills. In addition, the major image or paradigm for relationships in American life is *independence*. Even married people in their apparent union remain *independent*, married singles, as the Marriage Encounter movement calls it. Consultant and writer, Stephen Covey, says that there is a continuum of maturity -----> depen-

Patrick J. Brennan

dence ----→ independence ----→ interdependence. Covey says most would characterize maturity as *independence*, when in fact, interdependence is true maturity. Interdependence is the discovery of one's need for others, closeness, for intimacy, for synergy (or combined energies) when it comes to tasks or endeavors. We lock ourselves in and lock others out when it comes to communion and community.

Communion or community with others necessitates that:

1) we deliberately spend more *time* with people whom we claim to love;
2) we seek deliberately to understand the unique situations and circumstances of other's lives;
3) we keep commitments and promises when we feel like it and when we do not;
4) we practice honesty in communication, even if it is embarrassing because it is self revelatory, or challenging because it involves confronting another;
5) we apologize and seek reconciliation when we hurt someone;
6) we forgive someone who apologizes to us;
7) we encourage rather than discourage each other;
8) we pray *for* the people that we love; and pray for our perceived enemies;
9) we pray *with* the people that we love and pray with our perceived enemies;

10) we recover from the culture's approach to sexuality, and reveal its true nature and beauty. Sexuality ought not to be used to sell toothpaste, neither is it like shaking hands. We need to rediscover human sexual experiences as the deepest expressions of trust, commitment, and communication between two people.

Richard Westly wrote prophetically in *Redemptive Intimacy,* that true love requires a lot of unselfing, for human beings are naturally selfish. Susan Muto and Adrian Van Kaam in *Commitment: Key to Christian Maturity* say that to achieve commitment in relationships we stand in need of *grace,* for we are steeped in a culture of narcissism. Parker Palmer in *The Company of Strangers* says that concern for the other must transcend just our primary relationships, we need to practice mercy and compassion toward all — even strangers — the homeless, the hungry, the poor, the third world, different racial and ethnic groups. In 1987, the United States Catholic Bishops in *A Family Perspective in Church and Society,* call the Church away from its pre-occupation with the individual to become more an advocate for the *family* — blood families, single parent families, blended families, and families of choice, which most of us belong to in one way or another. *Home* is communion with others.

Home is not a place, it is the experience of communion with those who have gone before us in death. It is the realization we are still one with them in the

Spirit. It is the awareness that we can still speak to them and be heard, pray through them when we are in need. Sister Francesca Thompson reflecting on the life of Sister Thea Bowman said recently: God loved her so much He kissed her with a kiss that pulled her into total oneness with Him. For Sister Thea, who had a long bout with cancer, death was always the process of "going home." When the transition of death is reinterpreted for the self and others as "going home," our deepest fears are conquered; and we are truly free. Molly Fumia in *A Child at Dawn* tells the beautiful story of being paralyzed in life after the death of her infant son, until two years later she had a conversation with him on the profound level of her imagination. Mother and son reconciled and became one in the Spirit through the conversation. "I'll always remember and love you ," said Jeremy. "I'll always remember and love you, Jeremy," said the mother. Home is oneness with those who have gone before us.

Finally, home is living in communion with God, daily consciousness contact with our higher power. I have a reputation for being a high achiever, a very productive man. Without bragging, I can admit to being very disciplined, goal oriented, and productive. But I only do my many life tasks well, or with a sense of integrity and peace of heart when I am working a spiritual program. My program includes daily quiet time, prayer, writing in a journal, reading, exercise (running) and a certain amount of asceticism or self denial for a therapeutic purpose. When I work the program, or stay in communion with God, there is a power greater than I at work in me.

In summary, I try to do the best that I can in most endeavors, but I reach a point at which I turn it over, surrender it. Faith is the experience of being at home in the world with God.

A friend of mine is recovering from a bout with depression. Gradually as she has come out of the deep depression, she planned to take a job in another state. She took that job, but feeling herself sinking back into depression, she asked for a temporary leave and returned to Chicago. She visited me while she was in town, and told me of her deepening depression. I rather abruptly asked her "Where is your home?" She answered abruptly, "The southwest side of Chicago." She was even precise in naming the Church that she felt most comfortable in, and could pray well in. I told her, "Forget going back to the job. Stay here in Chicago."

That friend has begun to leave Oz and return to Kansas. Let us all, in a similar way, work our way back home.

Journal Questions for Individuals and Small Groups

1) Are you at home in the world? Why or why not?

2) Which of the 4 descriptions of *home* do you need growth in? Identity? Intimacy? Oneness with the spirits of deceased loved ones? Oneness with God?

Patrick J. Brennan

3) Do you provide *home* for others? What are your strengths as a source of *home?*

4) What are areas in which you, as a source of communion, need growth?

Chapter Eighteen

Beyond Impulse: On Discernment

WHEN I left my first assignment, as a priest, after seven years of ministry, I did no grieving. I celebrated my final mass there on Sunday, tearfully said goodbye to some friends at their home, and drove to my family home Sunday evening. I reported to my next assignment on Monday. I chose the parish without interviewing there, because they needed someone who had some skills in religious education. Not many parishes want or need priests in that area in such a large scale way; so, it sounded all right to me. During those days of transition, I was also asked to take on, in a part-time way, the directorship of the Diocesan Office for Evangelization. It sounded interesting, so I said OK. It was not long into the second parish assignment, that I began to realize that it is not wise to jump into a pastoral assignment, or any job for that matter, without some prior investigation, dialogue, and reflection. The new parish, while consisting of wonderful people, was something of a culture shock for me, it was radically different from the one I had been in. Ironically, I have stronger, more long-lasting relationships from that second assignment than I do from the first.

After getting a rather poor doctor's report on

Patrick J. Brennan

physical maladies arising from stress, I decided to leave the parish I was having trouble with. I named *it* as the source of all my problems. When news got out that I was looking for a new parish assignment, a pastor called and asked me to come and live in his parish. I could do minimal parish work, and focus more on my office. In typical knee-jerk fashion, I said yes. I gave no thought to how the move doubled my travel time to the Evangelization Office. Neither had I reflected much on how significantly altering the amount of pastoral work I did in a parish would contribute to even more depression. Parish number three eventually became a place of loneliness and isolation for me.

I am still at Parish three and the Office for Evangelization, eight years later. I hope what is apparent in the previous odyssey is *the lack of reflection* and *discernment* that went into each of those life moves. As I ran from parish to parish, accepted an office assignment, I paid little attention to my own inner world, the cultural realities of where I was moving to, or the needs of the people I was joining, and whether my gifts matched their needs.

After eight years, Parish three and the office have become home for me. After ten years with evangelization, two years part-time, eight years full-time, and after eight years in parish three, I began asking about six months ago, was it time to move on, perhaps to a pastorate? This time, however, instead of "running to the next thing," I decided to work a process, a pro-

218

cess of discernment, or sorting things out. At age 43, I know how accurate Carl Jung was when he said, in writing on mid-life, that one discerns in the afternoon of life, that the answers from the morning of life no longer work. Neither do the answers from the afternoon of life suffice for older ages of the evening of life.

Discernment had long been one of those buzz words that I heard at conferences, or in my work in RCIA; but I did not take it too seriously. I tried, as these issues arose, to consciously begin a process of discernment, to sort out, to listen: to myself, life, others, and God.

As I tried to listen daily to my own thoughts and feelings, I deliberately sought out the counsel of others. I talked with my pastor to check on his feelings about my becoming a pastor. I spent time with my long-time spiritual director. I talked with a clinical psychologist whom I respect. I spoke with my office staff; I also presented my searching to a board of advisors to our office. Finally, I wrote the Archdiocesan Personnel Board, expressing my interest in a given parish that was looking for a pastor, but also explaining the need for a transition time to secure a replacement for me as office director and to finish off some speaking engagements and other responsibilities attached to the office. Finally, one afternoon, I really felt *truth emerging* in me. I sat down and wrote the Cardinal all that was true, pro's and con's, about staying with evangelization work or moving toward a pastorate.

Though a few people, during this process of discernment encouraged me to "go for the parish," most felt the greater need was for me to minister to a larger audience via my evangelization work. I took their opinion as pieces of truth, but did not form any final judgments. I asked for an appointment with the Cardinal to discuss my letter. After listening, he said it was his opinion that the Archdiocese's greater need for me at the present moment was in evangelization work. After our discussion I informed members of the personnel board of the Cardinal's opinion, that I was leaning toward concurring with him, but asked if no suitable candidate could be found for the parish in question, that I be further considered. The board representative agreed.

Not too long after that it was announced that another priest was named pastor of that parish. I felt relieved that the whole process was over, happy for the new pastor, sad that I had lost "a child" (the parish), but confirmed that God seemed to be calling me in a certain direction, and I was willing to continue to try. I also was proud of myself for having worked a process of discernment rather than getting entangled in a process of impulsive reactions.

Discerning in a Non-Reflective Age

I often refer to Dr. Allan Bloom in my speaking and writing. In his book *The Closing of the American Mind,* Bloom speaks of how today's new openness has actually created a new "closed-ness." What has shut down is the mind, the spirit, the soul — and the ability to sift through, sort out, reflect, discern. There is little concern, he says, about the rightness and wrongness of things. The addiction experts warn that one of the primary American addictions is busyness addiction, wherein we try to fill the loneliness hole in our hearts with activities and things.

During a recent ride home, after delivering a talk, I inadvertently tuned in a radio talk show that described the rather expansive business of male prostitution that takes place on Chicago's north side. The author of a study on the topic explained how many of the male prostitutes, some in their teens, are not homosexual in their orientation; much of the activity is not about sexual gratification at all. Many, rather, are the products of dysfunctional homes, supporting their families by hustling their bodies. It is a matter of money, in other words. The radio interviewer confessed that until this interview, she thought any sexual activity between two relatively mature, consenting human beings was all right. Now, however, she was horrified at what she was hearing. Now she could see that all sexual activity is not *carte blanche* OK. I, myself, was overwhelmed with the description of systemic sin, societal sin, not only not reflected on by that interviewer, but also by me. The interview was an awakening experience for those on the radio and those listening to become more reflective, discerning people.

In a similar view, I recently spent time with an adolescent in family therapy. One of the presenting issues is that the young man was involved in selling stolen material in order to earn extra money for his own dreams. The net worth of the materials involved came to over $6,000. Since the young man is a Catholic, I temporarily took off my therapist's hat to put on my minister's hat. I said "On a whole different level, do you realize that we are dealing here with issues of morality?" The theft of goods coming to that amount is what we call, in moral judgment situations, "grave matter," or serious sin. The young man who was tracking with me in the exchange of psychological jargon seemed lost, certainly not overly concerned or upset, when issues of morality were raised. He appeared not to even have the equipment, the interior tools to engage in a process of moral discernment or judgments of conscience.

I do not want this discussion to focus just on moral discernment. There are all kinds of discernment processes people need to engage in throughout life. In addition to moral discernment, there is vocational discernment, intellectual discernment, discernment of one's giftedness, or charisms, and others. But in whatever area of life we may be trying to sort out, sift through, discern, there are a couple of common major movements. It was to exemplify these movements that I told my own story at the beginning of this chapter.

1) *Listening to one's own inner word.* This is the first step in discernment — learning to listen to one's own thoughts, feelings, values, convictions, and morals — and to name them. Carl Rogers

used to speak of the experience of "getting congruent" with one's self. I believe he meant much the same thing as I do when I speak of listening to one's own inner word. Up until recently, when I seriously considered a shift in ministry, I ran from task to task, or did people pleasing. I certainly did not take adequate time to name my own internal dynamics. This, in fact, is the chief problem for most people coming into counseling or therapy. They come with symptoms that really are an outgrowth of being out of touch with their inner dynamics like hurt, anger, anxiety, depression, loneliness, and the like. In addition, so many people get trapped in meaningless work, going through the motions of various, thankless tasks, because no one ever helped them learn how to discern charisms or giftedness.

2) *Listening to the Outer World.* One's outer word refers to those forces or persons that serve as life-giving authorities in a person's life. No one can do discernment by himself or herself. One's inner word always seek confirmation or challenge in the outer word. For a Christian, one's outer word consists of the wisdom of Scripture and tradition, the input of a support group, or the responses of another person — a friend or soul friend, therapist, spiritual director, minister, or someone else who knows the person well. An "outer word person" need not be a person who is an intimate friend, in terms of mutuality, and

sharing. But the "outer word person" does need to know the interior landscape of the person's life somewhat well.

3) *Weighing Alternatives.* Whether it be vocational discernment, discernment of charisms. or moral discernment, a person in the discerning process is conscious of alteratives, choices and evaluates and weighs them in light of one's own inner word prompting, as well as input from the resources of one's outer word.

4) *Making Decisions and Taking Action.* Eventually one has to get off of the fence. Not to decide is to decide. In fact, one of the hallmarks of the morality of our age is to not deliberately intend, not to decide, not to commit. One of my graduate students at Loyola, from Ireland, commented in her final paper last semester on how many people in Western society claim to be believers, but at best are tepid or lukewarm believers, and also how much "believers" give their minds and hearts more to the values of the consumer culture than to the values of the New Creation, the Reign of God.

5) *Evaluating and Shaping.* Afraid of failure, we are often reluctant to look back, reluctant to learn from the process described above — maybe we discerned and acted wisely; maybe our listening to self was not adequate or the resources of the outer word were not helpful or not used prop-

erly. Maybe simply the circumstances of our lives have changed, and even a fairly qualitative discernment process demands a rather quick re-evaluation and change of life direction. Death, sickness, divorce, sudden geographical moves, all are examples of situations that can demand rather quick rediscernment. In that, we ought not to be afraid, on a regular basis, to take inventory in an evaluative way, of the multiple discernment processes that ought to be going on in each of our lives. As I said in the section on 12 step programs, inventory-taking on a moral level, is not something that we do once. It is something, 12 step wisdom says, that needs to be done over and over again. Even if we have made mistakes, the discerning person takes the mistakes and uses them for learning, and then, shaping the future course of one's life journey.

I believe the five steps, listed above, of listening to one's self, bouncing one's inner findings off of other resources — both people and tools of faith, taking time to weigh alternatives, deciding and acting, and engaging in ongoing inventory and discernment are steps that can be used in many kinds of discernment — moral, vocational, life direction, and in the discernment of charisms.

Discerning Charisms

A woman recently asked me, at a lecture series I was delivering in another city, whether I was a charis-

Patrick J. Brennan

matic. It almost seemed like she would not seek the counsel she apparently wanted if I did not belong to one or another *spiritual-political camp.* A few years ago I would have answered *no;* for, at the time, as a younger minister, I was deliberately trying not to be owned by any group or faction. But because I have grown in my understanding of the word *charismatic,* I answered recently "yes, I am charismatic." I have come to believe that all of us are charismatic, that is, all of us share in the power of the Holy Spirit. Baptism, Confirmation, Eucharist, ought to awaken us to the reality of these charisms. For some, in a quality RCIA process, there is quality discernment of charisms. But for most of us discernment or becoming aware of our charisms is something we do later in life, often after discouraging times of having to do things that we are not gifted for, or equally discouraging experiences of "sitting on our gifts" and not using God-given abilities.

I think even the most relevant, renewed parishes are not adequately helping people discern gifts for ministry, enabling all of the Baptized to consciously minister in either a parish-based program — style ministry, or the often more important ministries in neighborhood, family, and market place. We still do *"Price is Right ministry."* On that venerable TV quiz-greed show, potential contestants are encouraged to "come on down" to zealously compete for "things," if they guess their approximate value. In *"Price is Right ministry,"* we encourage people to "come on

226

down" and volunteer for tasks, often discerned by the parish staff as areas of need. Note: in such volunteerism which is the staple way of doing "lay ministry," in the best of parishes, little heed is given to what the one "coming on down" feels called to do.

In several conferences that I have given recently, I ask participants to listen to themselves and name ways in which they are gifted by the Spirit. I then ask them to go to an *outer word* authority to seek affirmation as to whether the discernment of their own giftedness was accurate. Following the suggestion of Loughlin Sofield and Caroll Juliano in their book *Collaborative Ministry,* I ask people in this inner word — outer word discernment process to look especially for "gifts of being," gifts that constitute who the person is, make the person who he or she is, gifts that are at the core of one's personality. These gifts of being — like listening, holiness, prayerfulness, healing — eventually are translated into gifts of *doing.* But to focus first on doing short circuits the emerging truth of how this person is one with, gifted by the Holy Spirit. It is amazing how often people are emotionally touched when their gifts of being are named, celebrated, and prayed over. The emotion is usually due to the fact that these gifts of being have been chiseled out over the years, through struggle, pain, loss, or grief. Often the cross in one's life is the greatest gift one person can give to another. The paschal mystery, going on in each of our lives, renders many of us a kind of "Everyman" able to be empathic with

Patrick J. Brennan

most fellow strugglers — empathic because we have been there too!

What Spirit-filled communities many of our parishes and institutions would become if we more deliberately engaged in true vocation work — not focused on what I compulsively want to do or some other compulsive wants me to do, but rather what God is calling me to, what the world is calling me to, and what I feel is the best use of my gifts. Such an approach would turn our church upside down. Not only would the ministry specialists — the clergy, religious, and credentialed — become less dominant, we might finally have true ministerial collaboration, that is co-laboring, communities.

At the conferences I mentioned earlier, I have met clergy and ordinary baptized people with an anemic, impoverished understanding of collaborative ministry. It is easy for lay people, getting into ministry, to become the same kind of elite specialists that people have always accused the clergy of being. Also, it is easy for an intimidated clergy to relinquish certain ministries to people who are so gifted, rather than naming their own gifts and hanging in there with people, ministering side by side in a true co-laboring, charismatic model.

To Live a Prophetic Message

To become more discerning in a non-reflective age, to discern gifts which necessitates saying yes to some calls and no to others, to seek interdependence and

228

collaboration rather than independence and success, have a rather muted appeal to the age and culture around us. I am convinced, however, that if more and more bodies that call themselves Christian or Catholic took time and made the effort to embody discernment, charismatic living, and collaboration, we would be living a prophetic message more important than some of the tasks that we busy ourselves with.

Journal Questions for Individuals and Small Groups

1) Spend time doing some inner word listening — either regarding matters of morality, vocation, life direction, or charisms. What do you hear within?

2) Whatever you have heard in 1), share with Jesus in an imaginary dialogue. Journal what you think Jesus would say to you. Would he confirm or challenge your listening?

If in a Small Group or with another:

3) As individuals, do (1) as listed above.

4) In pairs, or triads, do actual affirmation or challenge with each other. Remember to emphasize gifts of being. Make sure to point out gifts people fail to see in themselves. What facilitates or blocks collaborative ministry in your parish or institution? What could you do to change non-collaborative models?

Chapter Nineteen

KATE: Good Grief!

A Saturday Morning

IT WAS the Saturday after Thanksgiving, early in the morning. I had stopped early at my mother's home to check on her needs before I went on to begin a morning of counseling at a clinic where I help out part time. My mother alarmed me in that she was sitting, literally draped on a chair, with a cordless phone in one hand. At first, I thought something had happened to her. "What's wrong?" I asked. "Kate's dead!" she gasped.

I held my breath, not wanting to alarm my mother more, myself stunned. "Kate" and "death" seemed like mutually contradicting terms. Though she was about to turn 91 in three weeks, she showed no signs of weakness or slowing down, except for sight and hearing deficiencies. "Kate — dead": impossible. She was there at our home less than 48 hours before, celebrating, declaring it the best Thanksgiving of her life. Kate: dead — oh, no; she was my favorite aunt. I was confronted with another loss; and I was, I am, so tired of losses.

Through a series of phone calls, I learned that indeed Kate had passed away. She had taken a bath on Friday night and gone to bed. The medical personnel reported that she had a massive heart attack or heart failure that took her quickly without much apparent pain.

Again, I was responsible, with the help of my brother and aunts, Lorretta and Monica, to go through the steps of funeral arrangements. More than with my father's arrangements, I sat stunned in the funeral director's office, as we began the rather sobering process of picking a casket and other funeral items. With my father and others, the gradual decline of their health made death more expected, if not acceptable. I began in that funeral home to experience some of the feelings associated with sudden death. She was there some hours ago; and gone now. My brother said it was like getting hit in the face with the back of a shovel.

Unconditional Love

People look skeptically at me when I speak of how much losing Kate hurts me. It is not that I do not believe in eternal life. Also, I thank God for the painless transition my aunt had. But in my family system, Kate was unconditional love for me. It seems growing up, even extending into adulthood, I tried to *earn my father's* love, or *please my mother*. There must have been *subtle competition* between two young males as close in age as my brother and I. But Kate visited weekly when we were children. And her visits were magic times for me. They were magic because I did not have to "earn," "please," or compete, with

Patrick J. Brennan

her. She just loved me, loved me unconditionally.

When I was young, I had terribly disabling asthma. My difficulty breathing prohibited my participation in many competitive sports. I found my fun in introverted ways, one of which was the hand-printing of a weekly newspaper. I called it *The Weekly Flyer.* Kate was my first and most long-lasting subscriber. Similarly, on Wednesday afternoons when we parochial school children were dismissed so that public school children could be catechized, I used a fragile toy radio station to broadcast a radio show from my bedroom to my kitchen, where my mother usually did the ironing on Wednesdays. Over thirty years later, I find myself spending a great deal of time both writing and doing radio broadcasts. Kate and my mother helped me to discover gifts that I never knew I had, gifts that I am still developing, with God's help, today. Kate was one of those special people who "helped me to like me," when I did not like or love myself.

Thus, Kate's sudden departure voided out some of the magic of my boyhood, a magic that had endured through adolescence, young adulthood, and middle age. Kate had continued to be at Thanksgiving, Christmas, Easter, the Fourth of July, and summer vacations to Lake Geneva, Wisconsin. She was always there, with her outspoken political and religious views, yet, also, her innocence, and her undying, unconditional love. Even at that last Thanksgiving dinner, her comments were such:

"Pat, take some time off; you need a rest."

232

PASCHAL JOURNEY

"Promise me that you'll take care of your Aunt Lorrie."

"Watch that baby, Katie." — my brother and sister in law's infant daughter, named after Kate.

And her final evaluation: "This has been the best Thanksgiving of my life."

Kate's lifestyle was a good prescription for all of us: hard work, physical work until her 91st year; exercise, mile-long walks; prayer — blocks of significant time each day; Eucharist — despite often inclement weather; and a focusing off of the self, and on to others in a spirit of selfless love.

On Grieving

Kate's transition has precipitated a lot of inner pain in my life. I miss her. It hurts. She was such a pillar of our family, I cannot believe that she is no longer with us. The only comparison that I can make to how it feels is that her death was and is like a rolling snowball containing within itself all the losses that I have experienced recently — family home, father, friend — and those that lie ahead and which I fear and dread.

On hearing of her death that Saturday morning, I rushed to her home to bless her body and kiss her good-bye. A hearse had already taken her body to a local hospital for her to be declared dead. I knew what I had to do — I had to be with her — her physical remains — before a funeral director began his work on her. I raced down south California avenue to Little

Patrick J. Brennan

Company of Mary Hospital, and caught up with the hearse, at the emergency room entrance. I asked the funeral director if I could bless and say good-bye to my aunt. He opened the back of the hearse and I partially crawled in. He pulled down the sheet, and there she was — cold to the touch, looking like just another old lady to be declared dead by some doctor who did not even know her. I kissed her forehead, and said "You know how I've loved you!" I made the sign of the cross on her forehead. As I walked away, I began to cry. I kissed her again the morning before they closed the coffin. As with my father, I slipped a picture of myself into the coffin, with the words "Love, forever, Pat." As I told my spiritual director, both times that I kissed her, I felt I was kissing Kate good-bye, but also more than Kate — indeed, many of the people who made up the first forty-three years of my life.

Grieving Kate has convinced me that in most of my losses I have "rushed to the resurrection." As I mentioned also in my previous book, *The Purple Rainbow,* I tried to do the same with a friend of mine who struggled with a close friend's suicide. "Let's get this behind me," I think, all the while burying pain that will not go away, and which will demand to be dealt with at some time in life. Kate "dug up" buried hurt and made me feel it anew, along with the pain of her loss, and the impending pain of other losses.

I think somewhere in my training, I over-dosed on "stage theories," specifically that there are stages one experiences in the face of loss. Just as I am learning that I, we, must pass through the darkness of loss and death before there can be the transformation of resurrection, so also I am learning that grief involves chaotic dynamics rather than clear cut stages. I now have waves of loneliness for, and longing to see and talk to my father, a good year and a half after his death. I feel loneliness, sadness, fear of abandonment, anger, rage, loss, depression — then a spiritual presence of Kate and my father, a presence closer than physical presence ever was. But it is not clear! Often I am all over the lot. And the dynamics of grief have slowed me down a lot, with a poor attention span and lacking motivation for tasks. Though I eventually have to discipline myself to get to things, I am getting more comfortable "feeling what I am feeling," and lifting it up in conversational prayer, rather than burying it.

Divine Consolation

One winter evening, before evening appointments, I was jogging down Lake Shore Drive in Chicago, as I often do. Kate and other recent departed loved ones were in my mind. There was also the disappointment of a recent phone call with my mother wherein I was reminded that she was unhappy and I could not make her happy; she is chronically ill, and I cannot make her well. Call it mid-life limits, or the collapse of a Messiah complex, but I felt very sad about my mother and the difficulty of being in a caretaking mode with her. Where was all of this leading, all this sickness, all these past losses, all these coming losses? I felt like I had a hole in my heart.

So with the pounding of my feet on the sidewalk, I began to repeat over and over again, the prayer that rose from within my heart — "Spirit of God, fill the hole in my heart . . . Spirit of God, fill the hole in my heart. . . ." I repeated the short mantra-like prayer for the entire run. When I arrived back at the health club, a new peace was within me — a peace that still ached, but was also consoled, comforted with divine presence. I was re-awakened by that run of the need for deep, regular prayer for inner healing, and the need, also, for a spiritual program, that raises my consciousness to sensitivity to divine presence, and places me in daily conscious contact with the God of healing.

When someone leaves your life, psychically, there is a kind of "hole" there. It is a permanent wound that moves to scar tissue. One's life is not necessarily "wrecked," but definitely scarred forever. Only divine consolation can begin to ease the pain of the loss. The faith conviction that a loved one is in total communion with God is at the core of the consolation.

When Kate died, the remaining family, many of whom are senior citizens, asked me probing questions about where she was now — how her body was being buried, but supposedly her spirit is elsewhere. It seems like some seniors, who swallowed our faith tradition whole, without question, are living long enough to ask questions that adolescents have for the last 15-20 years asked.

"What is Kate's spirit?" one senior citizen friend asked? I stumbled through an answer. A person's spirit is the essence, the core of the person, it is indestructible. It goes beyond death. In spirit, we are the same — ourselves as individuals; but we are also different — glorified and transformed into a total oneness with God. There is the mystery: we are at once the same and transformed. Just as Christ was the same, yet transformed, and not limited by the parameters of His body after the resurrection, so will it be with those who die and rise with Him. We cannot take it much farther than that in the mystery of life, death, and resurrection. That hope becomes a conviction from which we will not budge, a conviction which lends meaning to all of the little deaths and the final transition of physical death in our own lives, and in the lives of those that we love.

Permission to Grieve

At a recent Sunday liturgy, the obvious theme that the Scriptures suggested was that of Christian joy. I began my homily that Sunday with some of the struggles that I have shared with you over Kate and multiple losses. I confessed to wrestling with depression and grief, but that I also was growing in the conviction that God is especially close to the broken-hearted, and that Paul's notion of "praying ceaselessly" can

Patrick J. Brennan

eventually lead one to joy amidst sorrow and loss. In fact, opposites are usually present with each other — fear and trust, light and darkness, birth and death, joy and sorrow. The one pole on the continuum almost reveals with greater clarity the nature of the other pole. The joy and healing God eventually gifts us with is *in the midst* of our struggle and loss. God's strength shines through our weakness.

The reaction of the congregation disarmed me. I had given the homily: 1) to witness to the power of God at work in my vulnerability; 2) to give those in the congregation who needed it, permission to admit to their own losses and grieving; 3) to share some of my own humanity, breaking out of the myths and stereotypes of clericalism. The homily did not go over well, and it was not because it was poorly written or delivered. People seemed to not want their "strong priest" to be weak, to be depressed.

"You have to be strong for us Father!"

"You have everything to be happy about; why are you depressed?"

"Cheer up; smile again!"

Maybe it was not just a "priest thing." Maybe we just do not know what to do with loss and depression in each other. Because we cannot fix it or get rid of it for another, we run from it, or offer some glib phrase that makes the grieving, depressed people feel even more alienated and alone.

Just as the dynamics of grief in a person move toward healing only when that person stops running

238

and moves toward the eye of the storm, so, also, friends and family cannot run away but move to the center of that storm: often, not to say anything, but just to "be with," and "mid-wife," the comfort and presence of God. We need to grow comfortable with the notion that grief can be good. There are different kinds of loss in life, relationship loss, the intrapsychic loss of hopes and dreams, material loss, role loss, functional loss, loss in systems and institutions. We should expect the wild dynamics of grief to be present in all of them.

A friend from a catechumenate team sent me the following prayer. It was on a greeting card. I thought it was touching, so I include it here. The author is unknown.

Prayer On Healing

One day I shall be healed. That surety keeps me going, Lord. How it shores up my sagging, drooping spirit!

Great God, through Jesus Christ You have revealed Yourself to be a God of the suffering. The Lord Jesus showed us ever so clearly that You are not a Divinity who watches suffering from the safety of some heavenly clime.

Rather, You have proven beyond any doubt that You are near to those who suffer. You do not merely observe our suffering indifferently from afar.

And someday You will explain to me and all of humankind of every age the "why" and the purpose

Patrick J. Brennan

and the necessity of all suffering. Of every little pain. Of every serious illness. Of every heartrending loss.

Our Lord Jesus Christ caused the deaf to hear, the blind to see, the lame to walk. He cast out evil spirits, giving His own in their place. He forgave sins, giving sinners His grace so that they would sin no more. It was this same Jesus in whom You were well pleased.

This is my assurance that I, too, shall be healed. The time and the place of my healing are hidden from my eyes. That Knowledge is part of the mystery of suffering itself.

Until my healing comes, Lord, give me Your grace so that I may accept my suffering. Give me your strength so that I will not despair. Give me Your love so that my suffering may bring me closer to You, the origin and source of all love.

Amen.

Journal Questions for Individuals and Small Groups

1) Name the greatest losses in your life. Did you give yourself permission to grieve?

2) Are there any buried feelings in you that need unearthing? and healing?

3) What are the losses the group may have experienced, as a group? Has the group grieved sufficiently, some of the changes in the *life of the group?*

Chapter Twenty

Comfort and Challenge

"Comfort, give comfort to my people', says God. 'Speak to the heart of Jerusalem and call to her that her time of service is ended . . ." (Isaiah 40: 1-2).

The Comfort

THOSE few lines from the Old Testament have long been favorites of mine. They sum up so much the difference that faith has made in my life. The paschal journey, the paschal mystery has been quite upfront and clear in my life. The struggle or death components have been quite real and painful. I have grown convinced of the wisdom of the Letter to the Hebrews, that as Jesus was "perfected" through his suffering and death, I/we also are being purified and formed by the struggle and suffering of our lives. I do believe we are becoming the "selves" God intends us to be.

Suffering comes in a variety of packages; sometimes it involves sickness, or emotional distress, or relational problems, or financial worries. What is crucial is that we approach these periods of suffering with the lens of faith, specifically the lens of the paschal/passage nature of things. Trying to do that over these past years, whether it has been through bouts with severe

241

Patrick J. Brennan

fear and anxiety during my twenties — which, by the way, continue dramatically today in the form of anxiety disorders; or through a lonely confrontation with celibacy and all of it's realities in my thirties; or dealing with grief, loss, and depression in my forties, I have always come back to the same realization. One cannot run from the cross. The mystery of suffering must be faced, entered into, in fact. In the entering in, to what often is felt to be a dark void, so often I have met God, the risen Christ, the Holy Spirit.

Suffering has been like love for me — both awe-ful, in the sense of containing awe-producing pain; and *beautiful.* During such periods I most have felt the presence and power of God molding and shaping me.

As for the nation, Israel, God has been *comfort* to me in the midst of loss, pain, and death. I remain a believer, often for selfish reasons, that is, for the *comfort* God's presence and the *promise* inherent in the life, death, and resurrection of Christ, and the life, death, and resurrection of all of us. "Because of Him, I can face tomorrow," says the old Protestant song. Because of the Father, Son and Spirit, I find profound meaning in life, suffering, and death.

The Challenge

But the older I get, I become more aware that faith can be mis-used just for self-nurture. Part of the downside aspect of the evangelical movement is that it has deteriorated for some into a "me and Jesus" privatistic psychic lollipop that some folks suck to just make

242

themselves feel better. Self growth and development is obviously one of the main arteries running through faith and a spiritual life. Comfort is one of the "pay offs" of faith. But I/we always need to take care that the comfort dimension of faith does not become spiritual narcissism or self centeredness. The spiritual journey is about more than my comfort during my life journey. Gospel living, as I have tried to indicate in different parts of this work, necessitates also being challenged by Jesus and His revelation concerning the Reign of God.

Part of the challenge of the gospel is to live a God-centered, God-anchored life. After I have been comforted, I find it easy to fall into typical American independence, feeling that I can do it all myself again. I am challenged, especially through the wisdom of twelve step processes, to always remember that I need that "Higher Power" and "daily conscious contract" to remain whole, sane, and happy.

Another challenge of the gospel, flying in the face of the post-Christian culture we live in, is to work at and stay committed to genuine community relationships. We each belong to a number of communities. We have different contracts with these communities, needs to be gratified by those communities, and different levels of commitment. As a Catholic Christian, I specifically need the challenge of being a responsible part of the large Eucharistic assembly, as well as a part of a small base community, as well as part of domestic community, that is part of a network of primary relationships. To truly live communion, the felt experience of community, is a challenge in a culture of independence and isolation.

The gospel challenges me, us further to be close, proximate to those with whom Jesus would spend most of his time — the poor, the oppressed, the broken. I hear too often, from myself and others a stagnant resignation, that there is not much any of us can do to improve the lot of the oppressed or the form and shape of society. As Jim Wallis, from the *Sojourners* community says, too many followers of Christ are spiritually lukewarm and politically conforming. The work of social justice must be something that is part of our prayer lives, our worship, and our personal spiritual program. The challenge of gospel living is to give alms, to become politically astute and politically active — not in the sense of partisan politics, but in the sense of transforming the world. As Thomas Groome, author of the classic *Christian Religious Education* has said, people of the Kingdom of God are people in the process of being redeemed, trying, in turn to transform society. Too many of us, too long, have operated out of a "City of God" ecclesiology that dichotomizes between what we do at Church and what is going on in our world.

The Challenge of Evangelizing the Church

Those of us remaining in part of the organized, mainline churches need to realize that we face a challenge of evangelizing the very structure of our churches. Specifically the Catholic Church needs loving confrontation regarding the systemic injustice present in its style of doing Church. The ignoring of the gifts of priests who have married, the unflinching stand against a married clergy, the institutionalized rejection of the gifts of women in leadership positions in the Church, the neglectful pastoring of people that results from localizing too much responsibility and authority in one man — the canonically appointed pastor — all are but a few examples of the injustice within the Church. Our great challenge as Church members is whether we remain co-dependent within a dysfunctional system, or step into prophetic living.

Jesus would never want us to be desolate; He is comfort for us. Jesus would never want us too comfortable; He is challenge for us.

To Be Comfort and Challenge

Part of paschal living involves a loving acceptance of the comfort and challenge of Jesus. But paschal living also involves incarnating, that is enfleshing His comfort and challenge and bringing it to others. That make take the form of a "churchy" ministry; it may also involve trying to be light and salt, a comforting and challenging presence to people in ordinary situations.

On the journey we call "paschal," may Jesus comfort us. May he never stop challenging us. And may we comfort and challenge his world.

Patrick J. Brennan

Journal Questions for Individuals and Small Groups

1) In what specific ways does faith bring comfort to your life?

2) In what specific ways is faith a source of challenge to you?

3) What is a viable counter-cultural challenge that a group could do toward societal or Church systems?

4) Who are the people in your life most in need at this time of God's comfort? How could you bring it to them?